Making Music
with a Hearing Loss
Strategies and Stories

Second edition

Edited by Wendy Cheng
and
Willa Horowltz, Au.D.

D1564908

Association of Adult Musicians with Hearing Loss

aamhl

proving the loss of hearing does not mean the loss of music

AAMHL Publications
Gaithersburg, Maryland, USA

AAMHL Publications
Gaithersburg, Maryland, USA

Library of Congress Cataloging-in-Publication Data
Cheng, Wendy W., Horowitz, Willa C, Au.D.
  Making Music with a Hearing Loss: Strategies and Stories,
  2nd edition
  ISBN 978-1-52384-808-9
  1. Music   2. Hearing Loss   I. Cheng, Wendy W.
  II. Horowitz, Willa C, Au.D.

Contributors

Brad Ingrao, Au.D.
e-audiology.net
Long Beach, California, USA

Marshall Chasin, Au.D., M.Sc., Reg. CASLPO,
Doctor of Audiology
Musicians Clinics of Canada
Toronto, Canada

Thomas Albrecht
Stuttgart, Germany

Shirley Allott
Victoria, Australia

Terry Bruton
Port St. Lucie, Florida, USA

Sharon Campbell
Pueblo, Colorado, USA

Jennifer Castellano
Thornwood, New York, USA

Kathy Castellucci
Orlando, Florida, USA

Shih-wen Angela Chen
Taipei, Taiwan

Wendy Cheng
Gaithersburg, Maryland, USA

Eva Costa
Faro, Portugal

Nanette Florian
Rockville, Connecticut, USA

Mischa Goelke
Hamburg, Germany

Angela Hill
Norfolk, Virginia, USA

Matthew Mack
Melbourne, Australia

Charles Mokotoff
Potomac, Maryland, USA

Dawn Mollenkopf
Kearney, Nebraska, USA

Renee Blue O'Connell
Charlottesville, Virginia, USA

Janice Rosen
Washington, DC, USA

Stephen Shey
Boston, Massachusetts, USA

Esther Sokol
Alpharetta, Georgia, USA

Angelika Wild
Hinterbrühl,, Austria

Nancy M. Williams
Fairfield, Connecticut, USA

Nobuyuki Yoshimoto
Shimonoseki, Japan

Jay Alan Zimmerman
New York, New York, USA

Contents

Foreword

In 2011, our Association published the first edition of the title you are now holding in your hands. It became one of the very few publications that explained in non-technical language, how the ear works in relation to music perception and the limitations of hearing aids for music performance. It concluded with 11 personal narratives, each detailing an unique journey on making music within the limitations of today's hearing devices.

So why are we doing a second edition? Given that our Association has a sizable number of profoundly deaf musicians who were utilizing cochlear implants instead of hearing aid(s), we began to envision publishing an expanded edition of our book. With this edition, we have added two more chapters on cochlear implants and their limitations on music performance. The number of personal narratives has expanded from 11 to 23, and now has a more international flavor as we sought to demonstrate that the journey to living a musical life is indeed an universal journey which is not limited to English-speaking individuals only.

Many individuals were involved in making this edition a reality. My thanks to graphic designer Linda Nie for designing the cover and formatting the book layout. I thank audiologist Esther Merz for introducing me to musicians with hearing loss in German-speaking countries; to Kinga Wolujewicz in Poland for disseminating our call for personal narratives to adult performers at the 2015 "Beats of the Cochlea" music festival in Warsaw for cochlear implant musicians; and to those that worked on translating personal narratives from German and Japanese into English.

It is my hope that this new edition contributes to the growing body of literature that helps audiologists and music educators understand how individuals young and old with hearing loss can integrate music-making in their lives.

Wendy Cheng
Founder and President
Association of Adult Musicians with Hearing Loss
Gaithersburg, Maryland, USA
May 2016

CHAPTER 1

Hearing

Brad Ingrao, Au.D.

The human auditory system is a complex system of harmonics, mechanics and neuro-electronics. Each component has a specific purpose, but like an orchestra, these work together to create more than the sum of the parts.

This chapter will step through the auditory system from the "outside – in" and describe the function of each part and how they contribute to the whole experience of hearing and understanding.

Anatomy

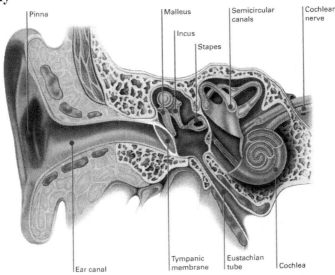

Figure 1-1: A cut away view of the outer, middle and inner ear. See text for more information. Figure courtesy of Bernafon-Canada. Used with permission.

The ear is divided into two major segments, the peripheral and central. The peripheral auditory system is further divided into the outer, middle and inner ear. Let's look at each part.

The Outer Ear

The outer ear includes the pinna and the external ear canal. These structures function primarily as funnels and resonators, but also protect the delicate structures of the middle and inner ear from foreign objects. In addition, the pinna is a great place to hang your shades during an outdoor festival, or to seat those fancy in-the-ear monitors you get when you finally get that big break. A bit more detail on each component follows.

The primary purpose of the pinna is to collect sounds in the air. Collecting sound energy over a large area and delivering that energy to a smaller area (the ear canal), increases the sound pressure of the sound. This increased sound pressure is perceived as an increase in loudness.

Take a look at your pinna. See all those ridges and grooves? Each of these diffracts (bends) sound differently depending on the frequency. This diffraction helps the brain make estimates of location, amplitude and phasing for the purpose of localizing sounds.

After being collected by the pinna, sounds travel down the external ear canal. This closed tube is about 2.5 cm long in adults and behaves acoustically like a single tube in a Pan flute (or empty soda bottle). The size and geometry of human ear canals results in significant resonant peaks at about 2700 Hz for adults and about 4000 Hz for kids. This ear canal resonance will come back into play later in this book when we talk about hearing protection. The end of the ear canal marks the border between the outer ear and the middle ear.

The Middle Ear

At the far inside end of the ear canal we find the tympanic membrane, or eardrum. The eardrum further amplifies the incoming sounds in two ways. First, it vibrates like the head of a tympani drum. You can argue the chicken and egg aspects of who named it first with your local anatomists and musicologists, and then let us know who won. The eardrum vibrates and moves three tiny bones, the Hammer, the Anvil and the Stirrup (Malleus, Incus and Stapes for you trivia buffs). This movement amplifies the sounds and passes them on to the inner ear. In addition, each of these bones acts as a resonating rod, with a different harmonic frequency. The eardrum also has a resonant frequency. The sum of all these resonances as well as the difference in area between the eardrum and the end of the stirrup adds about 31 dB to the incoming sound.

An important, but often forgotten part of the middle ear is the Eustachian Tube, which connects each middle ear to the back of the nose (nasopharynx). Under normal circumstances, the Eustachian Tube opens each time we swallow and re-equalizes the pressure in the middle ear relative to the outside world. This equal pressure is necessary for the eardrum to vibrate freely and for all the middle ear amplification described above to occur.

Eustachian Tube Dysfunction (ETD) is common in young children and people with chronic sinusitis. It causes a temporary hearing loss that affects lower frequencies more than highs, and results in a sense of being "plugged up" and having one's voice coming from deep inside a barrel. This is not necessarily an urgent issue, however long term, untreated ETD can progress to middle ear effusion, or fluid in the ear, and possibly a middle ear infection (otitis media).

For musicians, ETD can affect hearing overtones and harmonies, and can be painful for wind players due to the already high amount of intra-oral pressure needed to play. Clarinet and saxophone players will be further bothered by ETD since this "ear plugging" makes the sound of their instrument carried via bone conduction (teeth on mouthpiece) seem louder than the sound of their and other instruments coming into their ears.

Those with chronic ETD should consult an audiologist and physician to evaluate and treat the root cause rather than simply addressing the symptoms.

The Inner Ear
The base of the stapes, known as the foot plate, fits into a bony niche called the oval window. This opening into the inner ear is covered with a thin membrane and responds to the vibrations of the stapes. These then cause the fluid inside the cochlea, a snail shaped tube inside the temporal bone, to move. This movement takes the form of a travelling wave along the flexible basilar membrane.

This membrane separates the middle (scale media) and lower (scale tympani) tubes of the cochlea. All along the basilar membrane, rows of sensory hair cells make up the Organ of Corti. The structures of this organ transduce (convert) the vibrations of the basilar membrane into nerve impulses as follows:

Inside the Organ of Corti are thousands of sensory hair cells grouped in rows. At any given point of the organ, there are three rows of Outer Hair Cells (OHC) and one row of Inner Hair Cells (IHC). The OHCs act as pre-amplifiers, increasing the amplitude of the basilar membrane movements by contracting and expanding along their narrow tube-like bodies. This movement creates a sound, called the otoacoustic emission (OAE), which audiologists can measure and record. A second function of the OHC is to assist the brain in fine tuning pitch perception.

When a sound is heard, the brain records which OHCs and IHCs are stimulated and makes an initial guess as to the pitch of the sound. Then the brain "turns off" OHCs in areas just adjacent to the best guess "critical band." If the amount of nerve impulse stays the same, then the brain knows that the majority of the sound must have come from the best guess critical band. If, however, the amount of nerve impulse is reduced, then those adjacent areas must also contain significant energy and sound.

After a few of these "call and response" runs, the brain has a very accurate idea of the frequency of the sound, and then forms a perception of pitch.

Sounds great right? It really is unless we begin to lose OHCs due to age, disease or trauma (noise). When this occurs, the call and response system becomes confused because the brain never gets an updated attendance report when OHCs disappear. Loss of a few OHCs isn't a big problem, but the more you lose, the worse your pitch perception gets. For the average person, this means they mishear a few speech sounds. For musicians, this can be a career killer. We'll talk more about how to prevent OHC loss in chapter 2.

The second half of accurate hearing is the Inner Hair Cell. Regardless of the health and accuracy of the OHC system, the IHCs act like microphones, transducing (converting) the basilar membrane wave into nerve impulses. If the IHCs are also damaged, then, like a microphone with a torn diaphragm, the signal getting to the sound board (brain) will be distorted. No amount of amplification will "clean up" this signal completely; however certain technologies, which will be discussed in later chapters, will certainly help.

Central Auditory System
Almost home folks. Once the IHCs do their thing, the nerve impulse version of the sound we heard travels up the auditory nerve to several "weigh stations" in the brainstem. Here the signal is analyzed for timing, amplitude, loudness and pitch. The right and left ear's version of the sound are compared to determine location, and information is sent to, and received from, the memory, attention and emotional areas of the brain. Finally, the auditory cortex connects all the dots and declares that we've just heard A 440 and off we go to do it all again for the next sound. This finely tuned team works full time, 24/7/365 from the day we are born until we are laid to rest in a piano-shaped casket carried by aging rockers with gray "80's hair" and leather pants that are now a bit too tight.

CHAPTER 2

Speech, Music and Hearing Devices

Marshall Chasin, Au.D., M.Sc., Reg. CASLPO,
Doctor of Audiology

Music is everywhere - in the home, the car, the theatre, while jogging, and even when trying to study. Speech too is everywhere, and given a choice between hearing music and hearing speech, I suspect that everyone would choose speech. Communication trumps entertainment.

Many brain researchers argue that music helped to develop language, and language in turn, helped develop music. Identical parts of the brain are used when listening to speech and listening to music, and in fact, music can be thought of, as merely another form of communication.

Brain scientists have studied both speech and music and found them to be very complex. Neither is understood well. We do know that much of speech is located in the left side of the brain (at least for the majority of people) while music shares many of its function on both the right side and the left side of the brain. The part of the brain that joins the left and right sides (called the corpus callosum for those Latin scholars among us) is actually thicker in musicians than non-musicians attesting to the possibility that the interplay between the two sides may be a busier highway than for non-musicians. And, music tends to be routed through more "emotion centers" in the brain (such as the amygdala and certain parts of the cerebellum, again for those who like Latin). Loud music, and certain types of music elicit an emotional response that is sometimes missing with speech. Thankfully, we don't have to choose between music and speech.

Although the brain is rather complex and we don't fully understand how we process music and speech, we know many things about the differences and similarities between music and speech.

The loudness of speech at about 3-4 feet is about 65 decibels (usually written as dB).

A decibel is a unit of the sound level or how loud something is. A whisper or the rustling of leaves is 20-30 dB, and a loud cymbal crash in an orchestra can easily be over 110 dB. A noisy bus or streetcar can be 80 dB, and a plane taking off (if you are unfortunate enough to be on the runway) is about 130 dB. The higher the number (in dB), the greater the sound level, and the greater the potential damage to one's hearing. This is why hearing aids and cochlear implants provide sound that never exceeds an uncomfortably loud level. Its important to make speech and music loud enough to hear, but not too loud.

Rock and Roll needs to be loud!
Many people like music that is very loud. Part of the reason is that certain types of music (such as rock) need to be loud, whereas other types are intended for a less noisy venue. Another reason is that louder sounds (whether its noise or music) can cause the emotion centers of our brain (such as the amygdala) to become quite active. We have all heard a gradual welling up of a crescendo as the music comes to a climax, and depending on our personalities, we may have a tear in our eye. Yet, if music (or any noise) is too loud, it can potentially damage one's hearing. Also, loud music doesn't sound as clear- if music is turned down, our ear's natural ability to focus or tune itself, is improved. If the music is too loud, its as if the radio station has been tuned to slightly off the radio station. It may be loud, but will be fuzzy. (see Figure 2-1).

How then can we ensure that loud music is indeed heard through hearing aids or cochlear implants as sufficiently loud, but not too loud? And how can we ensure that softer sounds are heard as soft, but not too soft?

Figure 2-1: This blurred radio is a metaphor for how speech or music would sound if the volume was too loud. Our hearing mechanism simply cannot handle overly loud sounds without some distortion. Used with permission, Musicians' Clinics of Canada (www.musiciansclinics.com).

Compression and hearing aids:

In order to ensure that sounds are loud enough, but not too loud, hearing aids and cochlear implants use a system called "compression". This is not new to the hearing aid industry. Compression has been used with hearing aids and in radio and television since their onset.

Compression essentially means that soft sounds are automatically made louder and loud sounds are automatically made softer. Compression is sometimes called 'automatic volume control", or "automatic gain control". Virtually all hearing aids and cochlear implants use some form of compression. And according to the research, while there are subtle differences between speech and music, the compression circuit that is set up for speech is actually also quite good for listening to, and playing music. A major difference however, between speech and music is that music is much louder than speech. The loudest shouted speech is typically less than 85 dB, and this is mostly for the vowels such as 'a' in the word 'father'. A level of 85 dB is about the loudness of a dial tone on a telephone, and while we would not like to listen to this for every moment of the day, its not too loud. In contrast, even very quiet music (classical, jazz, or even soft rock) can be well in excess of 85 dB. Its not unusual to listen to your favorite song at 100 dB or even higher.

The limits of modern hearing aids and cochlear implants:
All hearing aids and cochlear implants are similar in the sense that they all have microphones, amplifiers, and have some way to transmit that amplified signal to the ear. In the case of hearing aids, the amplified signal is sent to a small loudspeaker (called a receiver) that either sits in the ear or is joined to the ear by an earmold, if the person is wearing a behind the ear hearing aid. In the case of a cochlear implant, the signal is transmitted through the skin to a small array of electrodes that have been surgically implanted in the inner ear. In both cases, sound enters the hearing aid or cochlear implant, is made louder in a manner specific to the needs of the individual, and is then sent to the ear.

The microphone is a wonderful device that has been around since the later part of the 19th century, and like many inventions, has gone through a gradual evolution. Microphones are devices that convert sound (or music) to electrical impulses that can later be amplified. Modern hearing aid and cochlear implant microphones are very sensitive and can transmit sounds as quiet as several decibels, and also can reliably transmit sounds as intense as 119 dB. A level of 119 dB is actually quite loud and typically heard as the louder parts of rock concerts or symphonies. Since the loudest parts of speech is much less than 119 dB (and is typically less than 85 dB) speech through a microphone poses no problem. However, very loud music can sometimes overdrive the microphone causing distortion with a resulting fuzzy sound. In the vast majority of cases however, music and speech can reliably be transmitted through a modern microphone with no ill effects.

Almost all modern hearing aids are "digital". This means that after the microphone but before the amplifier, sound energy is chopped up into tiny portions and each one is assigned a value depending on how loud each portion is. These values are stored as a number in a computer (inside the hearing aid or cochlear implant), and the process is called "Analog to Digital conversion" or simply A/D conversion. This is much like slicing a loaf of bread and dealing with each slice individually (see Figure 2-1). An A/D converter is very small and has no trouble fitting into even the smallest hearing aid or cochlear implant shell. In fact, in most hearing aids, there can be several A/D converters. The output of the A/D converter goes to the amplifier and this makes each of the millions of stored numbers in the computer louder (or softer) depending on the needs of the individual. Finally, this altered string of numbers is fed into a "Digital to Analog converter" (D/A converter) and sound (if a hearing aid) or an electrical signal (if a cochlear implant) is directed to the ear. In other words, we need to put the modified sliced bread back together again before we send it onto the ear.

Figure 2-2: In the Analog-to-Digital (A/D) conversion process with digital hearing aids, sound is chopped up into many pieces (or slices of bread). Used with permission, Musicians' Clinics of Canada (www.musiciansclinics.com).

Two reasons why A/D converters have a limitation:

It turns out that most hearing aid and cochlear implant engineers design these devices to prevent louder sounds from getting to the A/D converter (just after the microphone). There are two reasons for this. The first is that even though the microphones can reliably transmit sounds up to 119 dB, the A/D converter cannot handle sounds this loud. Usually a clipper (which is like a low-hanging ceiling) is installed that prevents sounds over about 95 dB from entering the hearing aid or cochlear implant. This prevents overdriving the A/D converter and seeks to minimize distortion. This limitation of a 95 dB ceiling has no ill effects on speech, but can have dramatic negative effects for music.

Recall that the loudest sound of speech is about 85 dB, and since 85 dB is less than the 95 dB limit that many hearing aids and cochlear implants use, its like safely going under a bridge- 85 dB is less than 95 dB. It is convenient to think of this clipper or ceiling as a low hanging bridge and you are sailing under the bridge in a sail boat with a tall mast. If the bridge is too low (or your mast is too high) trouble will occur.

Speech has a "short mast" but music (which is characteristically higher than 95 dB) has a "tall mast". Speech can get through the hearing aid but music unfortunately will not be allowed to get past the A/D converter bridge without distortion. The second reason is historical. Many hearing aid design engineers set this bridge (even before hearing aids and cochlear implants were digital) at such a low level because they were mostly concerned about speech, which is inherently quieter than music. Shouted speech simply cannot reach the level of the bridge.

Perhaps because of the demands of the baby boomer generation, non-speech sounds such as music, are quite rightly, becoming more important. And its these louder music sounds that are distorted at the very beginning of the hearing aid or cochlear implant amplification stages. Once music is distorted, there is no fancy programming or circuitry that can undo the distortion. The distortion of loud music needs to be addressed before it occurs.

Five strategies:

1. The simplest, and one of the most effective strategies to improve the clarity and fidelity when listening to music is to turn down the volume of your stereo or MP-3 player. (See Figure 2-3)

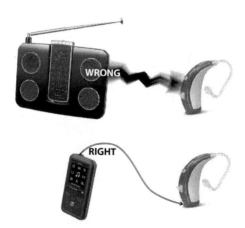

Figure 2-3: Because modern digital hearing aids and cochlear implants cannot handle overly loud inputs, the best strategy is to turn down the volume of the stereo or MP-3 player and turn up the volume of the hearing aid or cochlear implant (if necessary), not the other way around. Used with permission, Musicians' Clinics of Canada (www.musiciansclinics.com).

This allows the music to get in to the hearing aid or cochlear implant without its mast being chopped off by a low hanging bridge. The listener may still need to turn up the volume later on (after the sound has gotten under the bridge) in order to re-establish the desired loudness of the music.

2. Another modification to the way people listen to, or play music, is to use an assistive listening device such as an FM system. As the name suggests, an FM system transmits the music (or speech) using an FM radio signal. And like a radio, we need a transmitter and a receiver. The transmitter is a small box sized device with a microphone and is usually situated near the loudspeaker, or the person speaking. Regardless of how far the music or the person speaking is away from the listener, the sound is always received at a sufficiently loud level. This is where the receiver comes in.
The FM receiver is a small box (much like the transmitter) but can be either connected to the hearing aid or cochlear implant directly, or be used without a hearing aid. Your hearing health care professional such as your audiologist can assist you with the setting up of such a device. Typically, but not always, the music that you receive from this FM system is at a quieter level so the hearing aid or cochlear implant will not be overdriven. The speech and the music will be clearer with better overall fidelity.

3. A "low tech" solution would be to fool the hearing aid microphone into thinking that it is less sensitive than it really is. Placing a piece several pieces of tape over the microphone opening for example, would decrease its sensitivity, thereby providing more head room- the bridge has effectively been moved up while the tape is covering the microphone. This temporary change can be used whenever one wants to listen to, or play, louder music.

4. An even lower tech solution would be to remove the hearing aid while listening to, or playing music. While it may be true that you may require 30 or 40 dB of amplification, it is also true that you may only require a dB or so, if any, of ampli-

fication for music. Music is inherently louder than speech and your ear does not know whether the increased loudness has come from the hearing aid to your ear, or simply from the environment without a hearing aid. Removing the hearing aids would remove the low hanging A/D converter bridge problem.

5. There are now a number of devices on the market that look like a hearing aid, taste like a hearing aid, and smell like a hearing aid, but are not hearing aids- they are not intended for the hard of hearing market. These are called Personal Sound Amplification Products, or PSAPs. Some of these relatively inexpensive PSAPs can be quite useful for listening to music especially for those individuals that have a relatively minor hearing loss. Although PSAPs are not usually sold through audiology offices, your audiologist can suggest a model that may be optimal for music.

New technologies:
Another option is to discuss with your audiologist about a hearing aid that can handle louder music. This is not a "software" issue but is instead a "hardware" one. In other words, a hearing aid that can handle the louder elements of music is not a programming issue. The selected hearing aids must have this technology built in.

There are several technologies that are now on the marketplace and have been for the past decade. Some of these technologies raise the low-hanging bridge in the hearing aid so that even the louder components of music can get through the A/D converter without distortion, and other approaches use an analog compressor before the A/D converter and then digitally re-expands the music after. Both of these approaches work quite well for playing and listening to music.

Another technology that is more recent involves hearing aids that use 24 bit chips in their design. Without getting too technical, using a higher bit system allows this 96 dB ceiling or bridge to be increased to 110 or 115 dB- a level that is better suited to music. This appears to resolve many of the problems associated with the "old style" 16 bit systems that have been on the market since the early 1990s.

And one more thing ...
It appears that in trying to optimize a hearing aid for music there is an unexpected side effect- our own voice now sounds better through hearing aids. The level of a hard of hearing person's own voice, because its only inches from their own hearing aid microphones, can be quite loud and traditional hearing aids would distort their own voice. These newer hearing aid technologies not only improve the quality of music, but also the quality of a hard of hearing person's own voice.

The topic of music and hearing aids little to do with the software programming adjustments that an audiologist would make. It has everything with which hearing aids are selected for you.

And for a number of reasons, the optimal hearing aid programming settings for a speech-in-quiet program, are remarkably similar to those of an optimal music program.

CHAPTER 3

Hearing Protection for Musicians

Marshall Chasin, Au.D., M.Sc., Reg. CASLPO, Aud(C)

Introduction

Hearing loss prevention is the cornerstone of any hearing health care program. Although there have been amazing strides in our knowledge about how the ear and brain work, we are not yet at the point where hearing loss can be reversed. And even if discoveries are made, this is not something that will be accomplished in my lifetime. Reversing a sensori-neural (inner ear) hearing loss would require the same technology that would allow a person in a wheelchair to walk again. And it is never too late to start protecting your hearing.

Music, like speech, has energy over much of the range of the piano keyboard. Low frequency fundamental energy can be found for the bass notes on the left side of the keyboard and harmonics and higher frequency notes can be found on the right side. This is true of most musical instruments. Ideally, the best form of hearing protection would be to simply reach up and turn down the volume control knob such that all sounds are turned down equally. The relationship between the lower frequency fundamental energy and its higher frequency harmonics would be maintained. However, this ideal scenario cannot be achieved with standard hearing protection that was designed for the factory worker.

All hearing protection, including normal, industrial strength hearing protection has to follow the laws of physics. We all know that the acoustic impedance of the acoustic inertance is proportional to frequency…. Well, we don't really know that, but we can understand the English translation- high frequencies don't like small spaces or obstructions.

When a piano is played in a room and someone listens to it in the next room, the longer wavelength, low frequency sounds go through the wall almost unaffected. However, the higher frequency fundamental notes and harmonics on the right hand side of the piano keyboard are obstructed and attenuated by the wall. People in the next room hear the left side of the piano keyboard, but the right side is reduced in intensity. Unless something special is done to hearing protection or the walls in a room, the effect is that the balance of music (and speech) will be severely altered- low frequencies can still be heard well, but not the higher frequency energy of music or the higher frequency consonant sounds in speech. With conventional hearing protection music (and speech) will sound hollow, distant, and in the case of speech, unintelligible.

What then can be done? Short of appealing an ubiquitous law of physics- high frequencies don't like small spaces or obstructions- there have been some ingenious approaches around this problem. The most successful approach was introduced in 1988 by a company called Etymotic Research (www.etymotic.com). This book is not about any one manufacturer of products but this is a case where the world leader was, and still is, this one company. Based on some earlier research by an engineer named Elmer Carlson, on license, Etymotic Research came out with a custom earplug called the ER-15 (with the ER standing for Etymotic Research and the '15' being the amount in decibels that it attenuated or reduced all sounds equally by). The ER-15 takes advantage of some well known acoustic principles and in its design boosts many of the higher frequencies that would normally be lost to the listener. This essentially acts like a hand break against the earplug from cutting out too much of the higher frequency sounds. The net effect is a flat or uniform earplug attenuator that reduces all sounds (both the right and the left hand sides of the piano keyboard) by exactly 15 decibels. With this form of hearing protection, the bass still sounds like the bass, the trumpet still sounds like the trumpet, and the piccolo (unfortunately) still sounds like the piccolo.

Figure 3-1: A pair of ER-15 uniform attenuator custom made earplugs that provide exactly 15 decibels of hearing protection without altering the sound of the music. Figure courtesy of Etymotic Research. Used with permission.

At first sight, this does not sound like a lot and indeed clinically when I see musicians who are being fit with a pair of ER-15 earplugs, they do comment "is this all?" When it comes to hearing protection, more is not necessarily better. Fifteen decibels of hearing protection is actually quite enough for the vast majority of musicians and those who like to listen to music. The decibel is a rather complex measure of the intensity of the sound. It involves logarithms and reference points, dbut the bottom line is that a mere 3 decibel reduction in sound (which is almost not even noticeable) would cut the potential damage from loud music (or noise) in half. Another 3 dB reduction would reduce it one quarter; another 3 dB reduction (we're now down to 9 dB in total) would reduce it to one eighth; another 3 dB to 1/16; and finally another reduction of 3 dB to 15 dB overall, would reduce the potential damage from music (or noise) to 1/32.

This means that a 15 dB reduction in sound would allow a person to be in a loud musical environment for 32 times as long without damage to their hearing, as a person who was not wearing any hearing protection.

The logistics of obtaining a pair of ER-15 custom made earplugs is to make an appointment to see an audiologist. Other than having your hearing assessed, they can make custom earmold impressions of your ears and will send that to a local earmold laboratory. This would be the same laboratory that makes earmolds for hearing aids. About a week or two later the custom made ER-15 is ready to be fit. The material of the mold is flesh colored and typically made of medical-grade silicon. Ideally when fit, the musician should forget that there is anything in their ears and music will sound like it was without hearing protection but now will be safe to listen to.

By 1992 it became apparent that our percussion colleagues occasionally required slightly more hearing protection than the ER-15 and the ER-25 was created. As the name suggests, this provides 25 decibels of hearing protection which is identical for all sounds. Without wading through the math, a typical drummer would be able to play his or her instrument about 256 times as long before the same damage occurs as a drummer who was not wearing hearing protection.

Not everyone wants a pair of custom made earplugs (at a cost of $200 - $250) so the ER-20 was invented. This one-size-fits-all earplug, provides hearing protection that is somewhere between the ER-15 and the ER-25, but sells for a fraction of the cost of the custom made earplugs. The ER-20 has recently been re-named ETY• plugs and is shown is figure 2. These actually come in a range of colors and several different sizes.

Figure 3-2: The ETY•plugs which are non-custom and one-size-fits-all. Because one size does not really fit all, the ETY•plugs come in different sizes. Figure courtesy of Etymotic Research. Used with permission.

Other manufacturers have recently come out with similar devices- hearing protection that is uniform or flat and treats all of the sounds similarly, and information on these can be obtained from your local audiologist. Some look similar to the ER-15 while others are unusual shaped headsets that have bunny eared "side resonators".

Hearing aids and hearing protection

Can my hearing aids act as hearing protection, or since I already have a hearing loss do I still need hearing protection? The answer is yes, and yes. Although it is not straightforward, research performed in the 1990s did show that a person with a hearing loss is no more, nor less susceptible to further music or noise induced hearing loss than someone with normal or near normal hearing. So, hearing protection is important for everyone.

Depending on the exact nature of your hearing aids, they may be protective. Some can be set to provide "negative amplification" or hearing protection if the sound in the room is too loud. This may differ from hearing aid to hearing aid, and from one hearing aid fitting to another. It is best to consult your local audiologist for more information with your specific hearing aid fitting. And what about the earmold – the piece that joins the behind the ear hearing aid to the ear? If there is no air hole or "vent" in the earmold, then this can function quite well as an earplug. If there is a sizable vent in the earmold, this will limit the usefulness of your hearing aid as a hearing protector. Again, it is best to consult with your local audiologist about this issue.

CHAPTER 4

Programming Considerations for Musicians with Cochlear Implants

Brad Ingrao, Au.D.

The programming of a cochlear implant is considered by many to be akin to magic, but it is really quite clear cut. The goal is to provide the recipient with access to a range of sounds at 20 to 25 dB (a whisper at 3 feet), which is the new electrical threshold, and to prevent loud sounds from exceeding the recipient's limit of comfort. The space between these levels is called the dynamic range. Unlike hearing aid users, the cochlear implant user has a bit of an advantage since the audiologist can create a dynamic range that ideally accommodates all of average speech and most environmental sounds. While different manufacturers provide slightly different sized dynamic range options, they all have the limitation that they are designed for speech. This allows the majority of CI recipients to rejoin the world of human communication quite effectively after a year or so of habilitation, but what about music?

As Dr. Chasin discussed earlier, the physics of speech and music are quite different. Just as hearing aids have inherent hardware limitations when it comes to processing sounds louder than typical speech, so do cochlear implants. Like hearing aids, each CI processor has a slightly different input limiting threshold, but in general, you can assume that if the music you are listening to or making is louder than a typical raised voice at 3 feet, your hardware will create some amount of distortion which may degrade the quality of sound. As with hearing aids, the best way to combat these hardware limitations is to control the input level to the microphone.

A very easy way to do this is to use a smartphone app to measure the sound pressure level. There are several free "Sound Level Meter" apps for both Android and iOS. These are accurate enough to give you a ball-park estimate of the incoming sound. Once you have installed the app, start measuring and ask a friend or family member to count out loud and incrementally raise their voice until you just begin to hear a quality change.

This will usually signal that the sound level of their voice has reached the input limiting threshold of your specific speech processor. Once they reach this level, make note of the number on the app. If you now keep the music you listen to or make just below that level, you will be able to control one of the limitations of the hardware as it relates to music. The second hardware limitation that exists in cochlear implants is the finite number of electrodes on the internal array. Even with the most advanced virtual channel technology (current steering), the average CI recipient will only have access to 120 discreet frequencies.

It is true that in one study, some Advanced Bionics HiRes Fidelity 120 users could hear over 400 pitches, these results were obtained using a research version of the software, not in the final product, and should not be considered a reasonable expectation for most users.

If we assume the best typical case of 120 pitches across the electrode array, and the typical frequency coverage of 330 to 6700 Hz, we can make some better choices about the music we make and listen to. A very helpful interactive map of the typical frequency ranges of most modern instruments can be found at http://www.independentrecording.net/irn/resources/freqchart/main_display.htm.

This page allows you to point to an instrument and a window reveals the typical range in Hertz. If that instrument's range falls within the CI range above, it can be considered a "possible" instrument to hear under the best case scenario. This should be considered a very rough estimate and in no way should be considered a guarantee that a given instrument within that range will sound well or familiar. The overtone characteristics of many instruments are much more complex than a cochlear implant can resolve accurately, so as with everything in hearing, your mileage may vary.

While there is not "magic formula" for programming a CI to maximize music enjoyment, a few general ideas apply. Most of these relate to the KISS (Keep It Super Simple) principle. In recent years, cochlear implant processors have begun incorporating front-end processing similar to that available in hearing aids. These processes are attempts to "clean up" the speech signal in order to maximize speech understanding. These generally focus on adjusting the sensitivity of the microphones and attempting to reduce environmental sounds that are likely not speech. This is great when you are in a windy or noisy environment, but these same features will often identify music as non-speech and distort or reduce your ability to hear it.

If your CI's version of these front-end processing is making music sound strange, you can discuss creating a program that disables these features while providing the maximum available dynamic range. This in conjunction with controlling the impact of input limiting is really the best we can do to feed your CI a music signal that is as compatible as possible to the hardware limitations of a CI.

A recent advancement in cochlear implants is the addition of an acoustic component to the CI processor. As of the time of this printing, only the Cochlear Hybrid is FDA approved for use in the US, however MED-EL has offered its EAS system in Europe previously and Advanced Bionics is working on a similar system. The concept of "hybrid hearing" is to use a power hearing aid speaker to provide acoustic hearing for low frequencies when post-operative residual hearing below 1000 Hz stabilizes at better than 60 dB HL.

This low frequency acoustic information is helpful in localization and for parts of the "speech in noise" picture, but also provides a more "natural" appreciation of some music. For those who are not candidates for hybrid hearing, the use of a conventional hearing aid on the non-implanted ear can provide some of the same benefits.

The final technical piece of the CI music puzzle is practice. There are several music rehabilitation programs available through the CI manufacturers. I deliberately avoid mentioning them here because as with everything else technology-related, they change. These are available from your audiologist who will have access to the most current versions. We'll discuss more details of this process in the next chapter.

CHAPTER 5

Grieving "The Way We Were" and Learning to Love "A Brand New Day"

Brad Ingrao, Au.D.

Despite all the wonderful advancements in cochlear implant technology and rehabilitation, the unfortunate reality is that music will never sound the same as it did before your hearing loss. Take a moment and let that really sink in. Now take another moment and allow yourself to get mad about that. Losing hearing, particularly for an emotionally significant experience like music is the same as having a friend or family member die. Like a death, we must grieve it. Susan Kubler-Ross' work "On Death and Dying" outlines the now famous stages of grief: Denial, Anger, Bargaining, Depression, Acceptance. Many of you have already traveled this path in regards to your hearing loss in general, but music is such an emotionally-loaded experience, especially for performers, that it requires its own grieving process.

Over the years, I have encountered many people who seem to have really found peace with hearing loss as it relates to speech. I suspect this is due to the fact that hearing aids and cochlear implants have improved to the point that for most, speech in quiet is very accessible, and speech in moderate noise is at least a possibility with some additional logistical and technological assistance (careful positioning relative to noise, the use of remote microphones, etc.).

Because these truly remarkable devices were not designed for music, especially live music, nearly everyone will face the reality that their function in this domain will be poorer than for speech.

If you are reading this book, chances are quite high that you fall into this second group. I wish with all my heart that I could tell you there is a programming trick or new gizmo that will "fix" this, but as George Washington is reported to say, "I cannot tell a lie." What I can provide is a plan to repair your relationship with music and hopefully, lead you to finding your next Beatles, Vivaldi or Dave Brubeck.

Saying Goodbye
As a musician myself, I realize that a huge part of my relationship to certain genres is how the notes, chords and harmonies combine to create emotional responses in my body. Some of this is predictable and planned (minor and diminished keys vs. major keys), but some is very individual and personal. This seeming duality offers you a unique opportunity to find new music to listen to and play that is more compatible with your hearing and hearing technology. By focusing on how music makes you feel rather than what it sounds like, you have the opportunity to build new musical friendships. The following is one suggestion for opening yourself up to new options. If it works for you, great. If not, try to glean some of the fundamental ideas about letting go and find your own way back to the music.

The One-Year Plan
Before you can find your new musical posse, you have to bury and cry for the old. Select your ten favorite pieces of music and listen to them in the most ideal conditions for your cochlear implant.

This means being in a room with good acoustics (carpet, low ceiling, drapes, etc.). Play the music through the best quality sound system you have access to and control the output so that it reaches your cochlear implant microphones at less than 85 dB SPL.

For pieces you used to play, pull out the sheet music or score and read along. After each piece, write a list of all the emotions you felt during the piece. Repeat this for your next 9 favorites.

After you complete the list, pack up the music in a box, seal it with packing tape and stash it in a closet where it's really hard to get to. Set a reminder in your smartphone to open the box in one year.

Now, have a really good cry. Get all the anger and sadness out. Tell yourself that you WILL find other music that moves you and that you will NOT dwell on the past or compare any new music to your "top 10."

After the catharsis (you may have to repeat a few times), head down to the local used music store, or sign up for one of the many streaming music apps like Spotify or Rhapsody.

Randomly select to songs and listen to them under the same ideal conditions as above. If any of them evoke the emotions on your list, mark it down next to the emotion and move on to the next song. You may have to go through several 10-song cycles before you hit fill up your new hit parade, but keep at it. After you find to solid songs that make you tap your foot like the old days take a moment and reflect on what has happened. Even after losing your hearing and having to re-learn to hear, music CAN and DOES move you. You are still connected to it, and it to you. Make this your daily mantra as you continue to explore new and different music.

After the year is up, dig out the box, open it and listen to the old favorites again. If you have really allowed yourself to be open, they will have the same emotional hooks they always did and you will pay much less attention to how different they sound.

A few tips for helping this process be more successful:

Start with REALLY simple music like drums. Cochlear implants are really good at speech-like patterns. Drums are speech-like in this way and are very easily heard well.

Once you master non-melodic music, progress SLOWLY. This means reduced spectral and dynamic ranges and single instruments. Native American flutes are perfect for this step. They represent a limited diatonic scale and are acoustically similar to the vocal tract.

After this, pick your favorite melodic instrument and listen to acapella versions of music. From here, progress to simple accompaniment (single guitar, piano, etc.).

Slowly add levels of complexity as the previous level begins to sound "good" or "better."

Hopefully, this chapter has given you some ideas about how to re-connect with music after cochlear implantation. We can't make it like it was, but if you allow yourself to, you can and will find new songs and learn to truly accept the way your old ones new exist.

About Marshall Chasin and Brad Ingrao

Marshall Chasin, Au.D. has been the Director of Research at the Musicians' Clinics of Canada since the mid-1980s. He has presented nationally and internationally on hearing loss prevention in musicians, and fitting hearing aids on musicians. He has written or edited six books - three of which are on musicians and the prevention of hearing loss. Dr. Chasin received his Doctorate of audiology (Au.D.) in 2003 and plays the guitar, oud, and clarinet.

Brad Ingrao, Au.D. is an international lecturer and subject matter expert for academia and the hearing industry. Dr. Ingrao specializes in finding unique solutions for people in challenging listening and hearing settings. He is an expert in all major hearing aid manufacturers and certified to evaluate, program and troubleshoot cochlear implants from Advanced Bionics, Cochlear and MED-EL. Dr. Ingrao is an avid musician on the saxophone and enjoys working with musician patients.

CHAPTER 6

Personal Stories

Adult Musicians with Hearing Loss

Thomas Albrecht

Thomas Albrecht—Classical and acoustic guitarist
Stuttgart, Germany

My name is Thomas Albrecht and I live in Stuttgart, Germany. I teach classical and acoustic guitar for all levels and genres as well as piano up to the intermediate level.

As a child I had scarlet fever and lost a little bit of my hearing. I suffered a sudden hearing loss when I was 30 and also began dealing with tinnitus around that time. Time after time I would suffer temporary hearing loss, and my hearing would eventually return after each episode. I must confess, since the hearing loss was temporary and I hated sitting in an audiology booth listening to electronically generated beeps, I did not monitor my hearing loss very carefully and did not even see a doctor about it. I thought I could endure these episodes because I was able to keep up with hearing spoken conversations and heard my musical instruments rather well. (I have a wonderful Steinway piano and I also have a very expensive guitar made by Santiago Marin.)

I started piano lessons as a child. Then around the age of 15, I started to write songs, short stories and TV plays. During my college years, I have had quite some success as a songwriter and screenwriter. I wrote for a few TV films and was writing for the children' programs when I began to experience some burnout. I took a hiatus from writing and traveled around India for almost two years after graduation. Then I returned to Germany and decided to go back to music. I felt I loved music more than writing. I started learning classical guitar, which has had been a big dream of mine ever since I had heard someone playing Bach on the classical guitar.

A few years later, I started teaching music and giving music lessons. I was very surprised to find teaching music to be a wonderful and fulfilling profession. This discovery was totally out of the blue for me.

Until then, I thought, teaching might be boring and I started giving private lessons as a way of paying my student loans. But beginning with the first lesson I gave, I discovered that my real talent is to teach. I loved teaching much more than giving concerts. I loved playing classical guitar for myself but did not relish playing on a stage with many people present.

I soon discovered that to teach is a much different experience than to perform. To teach one needs the talent to meet each student at his or her level, and to provide patient instruction and proper motivation to help each student develop their skills, I love to work with kids, they are very fresh and energetic; but I also love to work with adults as well. It is completely wrong for mature adults to think they cannot learn as fast as my younger students; they can! My youngest student is 4 1/2 years old; my oldest students are close to 80 years of age. The mature student understand and grasps concepts much faster then my young students and they are incredibly thankful to find someone, who has the patience and joyful demeanor to teach them all facets of music from theory to performance.

However by the time I turned 50 years of age, I realized I was finding it much harder to understand people around me, including my students. I do not know whether the slow and now permanent deterioration of my hearing was due to advancing age, my tendency to attend loud concerts, or to the temporary episodes of hearing loss that I experienced before. It was around this time I met with an audiologist and received ear monitors and earplugs to protect my hearing.

As I approached my late 50's people started trying to convince me to obtain good hearing aids, but I was ashamed of my hearing loss. And because I was now a music teacher, I was afraid that I would lose my reputation as a good music teacher if I admitted that I had a hearing problem.

But, the treble voices of my female and younger students were giving me more and more problems. So I finally decided to try and obtain good hearing aids.

It is to be said that every new hearing aid user must go through an adjustment period. The first time I wore my hearing aids, I was really shocked at the cacophony of noise when I was hearing; after all my ears had been insulated against loud sounds in recent years. And the feel of the earmold in the ear was rather uncomfortable. Meanwhile, I had to remember to take off my aids before stepping into the shower since my hearing aids are not waterproof and I frequently forget that I am wearing them.

I think it took me close to a year to become accustomed to my new hearing aids . Actually, the adjustment period is for the brain, which has to learn again how to interpret new sounds just like a toddler---- to filter out, unimportant sounds and yet learn to focus on important information one needs to be aware of. I kept trying a few different brands and I must say, my musical instruments sounded terrible with many of the hearing aid brands. For a while, I lost all joy in playing my instruments. But after a really long time trying various brands, I found hearing aids which were perfect for me. They do have a special micro sensitivity of 120 db and after a while I changed the small speakers of them to the medium ones, to have more bass.

And I must say, it was a wonderful decision to obtain hearing aids. Of course, it's not the same as normal hearing, but now listing to music is really nice again. I can hear all the high frequencies again. My piano and guitar both sound wonderful and it is fun to play them again now.

My audiologist and I worked very hard at programming special settings for these aids: one program for listening to speech, one program with less amplification in the higher frequencies, and one program for music listening. As I said, it takes a really long time and a lot of work, but in the end, I am really happy with these aids and a bit regretful that I did not try hearing aids earlier. I am more relaxed . . . no longer do I need to bluff or pretend that I understand someone talking to me when I really did not understand their words.

Shirley Allott

Shirley Allott—Amateur harpist
Victoria, Australia

I was born with normal hearing, attended grade school and trained as a nurse. Music education was not part of my upbringing even though my father played harmonica and concertina and my brother learned the mandolin. I taught myself recorder and to read music and I sometimes played with my father and brother in family music sessions but my main interest was painting and textile arts.

When my children were finishing school I decided it was time upgrade my nursing qualification to the bachelor of nursing so I went to university and over several years completed a number of degrees in the health sciences. By this time, I was having difficulty in hearing, which made lectures and tutorials difficult to hear, but I still managed to do well. However I decided not to do a doctorate.

Both my older children at university became involved in historical re-enactment. I was fascinated and got involved too. With my knowledge of textiles I made costumes for others and myself. I went to a feast where I heard medieval music being played. I was spellbound and I brought out my recorder and started to play again. My daughter decided to teach herself violin and she and I played music together. She started to hold monthly musical sessions at her place with friends. My daughter knew I was now having difficulty hearing and she would always face me during those sessions. I really enjoyed these times.

I took up a new challenge, English concertina, a reasonably loud instrument, and went to Celtic Southern Cross Summer School. I experienced playing music with others and loved it.

Over the next couple of years my hearing loss markedly increased and I found myself withdrawing socially. I stopped going out with friends and going to gatherings. I was embarrassed, as I often had to ask people to repeat what they had said. I had looked into hearing aids but they were very expensive, far too expensive I thought. George, my husband, was very supportive and encouraged me to get hearing aids. I think he was finding communicating with me difficult. My first hearing aids were Oticon Pros.

There was a period of adjustment to the hearing aids and I could engage socially again but I found playing the concertina difficult.

I heard a different sound with my hearing aids and the concertina echoed. I wanted to play music so I needed to find an instrument that would work for me with hearing aids and to find a way of dealing with the change in sound.

At an event in Western Australia when I met a lady playing a harp and she invited me to try her harp. I realized as I plucked the strings that I could both hear and feel the vibration of the harp. I had bought a harp a couple of years previously at a folk festival but I hadn't done anything with it. I knew that when I got home I would learn to play my harp. I watched others playing harps, read harp books, and looked online, and practiced and got used to the sound and vibrations.

I found a harp teacher who helped me to understand harp technique, playing chords, and rhythm. I wanted to play music with others but I found sessions difficult as I find it difficult to recognize and distinguish pitch. I could only occasionally observe other harpists so I needed to find other strategies to allow me to play in an ensemble. I could read music but I understood very little music theory. I needed to know how chords worked so I read and studied everything I could in books and online.

I learnt how chords worked and chords that are used in different keys and how these were played on guitar so I could watch the guitars. I came to recognize change in vibration and tone with chord changes.

Rhythm has always been difficult for me. I tried using a metronome for rhythm and I tried an app on my ipad with a flashing light. Both needed concentration and I couldn't play while trying to hear a tick or watch a flashing light.

I found out about Community Music Victoria (CMV) not long after I started playing the harp and this has really been helpful. At CMV events I realized I needed to feel rhythm. Marimbas were so helpful. I didn't play one, but while others played I could feel rhythm as well as pitch through vibration. I love having marimbas, drums or a double bass at a music gathering because I can feel the beat so well. I learnt new ways of playing music and I gained confidence. I met many people with different skills and experiences.

With the skills and confidence I have gained I started playing with Christmas Hills Orchestra, a community orchestra which plays baroque and renaissance music. Now I have had the challenge of figuring out figured bass and playing with brass instruments which are loud. I watch the fingers of the keyboard player who is also the conductor as I play.

I learn by eye, and feel, and not by ear. Music notation for me is easiest but it is not always available. Through going to CMV events I have learned there are other ways of writing down a tune using letters or chord list on a piece of paper or on a white or black board. Sometimes another person writes down an outline of a tune and I copy it.

Technology is also helpful. I can photograph a tune on a board and I can make a film clip of finger movements on a harp with my iPad. I can later playback and slow down the film and watch as strings are plucked. I can also record a tune with an app which will give me an outline of the notation. Once I know how a tune goes and have played it a few times, I can play it without any notation, but not always as it is usually played. I continue to watch others and feel vibration and rhythm and if I know what is in the music, I can adjust what I do.

I am also learning to record a tune on my iPhone or iPad and play it back with using my hearing loop, which delivers the sound directly to my hearing aids. I am still exploring what I can do with this technology.

I replaced my hearing aids in 2014, about five and a half years after I started wearing them. I now use Oticon Alta Pro hearing aids and I am very pleased with them.

I spent time with my mother and played my harp to her as she was receiving palliative care. After she had passed away I researched how the harp could be used in Health care and found the International Harp Therapy campus with Christina Tourin. I have now completed the course. I learnt that as well as having a clear tone, the vibration of the harp is important in music therapy.

Being able to adapt and adjust to change is important in life. If my hearing had not deteriorated I may have continued at university and done a doctorate but I don't think I would have played a harp or done a harp therapy course or played with an orchestra. I am content with my musical journeys as a musician with hearing loss, and look forward to many more years learning and exploring music with my harp.

Terry Bruton

Terry Bruton—Amateur guitarist
Port St. Lucie, Florida, USA

I was born in November 1946 in Fayetteville, North Carolina with normal hearing. I can recall listening to music in our home in the 1950s. My mom, who is from Naples, Italy, would sing songs in Italian. My dad would sing American country songs whenever I rode with him in the car. We had a tabletop radio and eventually, an RCA console with that played 78 rpm records. I loved music from early on.

I think the first live performance I saw was at a country fair where I saw a band playing on a stage and was focused on one of the guys who sang and played guitar. One time, a symphony came to our school and played a concert. I was in awe of all the different sounds from the various instruments, wind, strings and percussion. That concert definitely made an impression on me.

We moved to Dania, Florida in June 1957, just before I began fifth grade. Once the school year began, I enrolled in the school band. I chose trumpet but ended up playing cornet at the suggestion of the band director as there were enough students playing trumpet and he really needed someone to play cornet. I continued playing in the school band until the end of the ninth grade. It was a great experience but I was into running on the track team by then and didn't want to be in a marching band.

After high school, I enlisted in the United States Air Force and joined a little band. We weren't great but practiced every chance we had and played a few places. It was fun. About this time, though, I noticed I could not understand all the words to some songs playing on the radio, tapes and records.

When I got married in September 1967, I would ask my wife to please write down the song lyrics for me if she could hear them. Once I saw the lyrics written out, then I could understand them more in the song because I knew what was coming. Remarried now, my current wife has impeccable hearing and helps me out quite often.

After I completed military service, I worked for an electric company and eventually started my own business. Individuals who do electrical work are often exposed to a lot of noise on the job. I'm sure we did not protect our hearing as we should have. Hearing conservation and the occupational hazard of overexposure were unheard of until the early 1970s, but the awareness of the dangers of loud noise was in its infancy and took awhile to get people to comply. Meanwhile, I continued jamming and playing music with some friends through the years and performed in public a few times. My hearing stayed about the same, with no real problem hearing people talk but I still had trouble with understanding some words in songs.

By December of 2005, after 30 years in the electrical business, I moved on to work for the city of Port St. Lucie as an electrical inspector. After about five years, I could sense I was starting to have problems understanding words in conversation. Even as an inspector, I was subjected to industrial noise. I had my hearing tested and I was found to have mild to moderate hearing loss in the lower frequencies and severe hearing loss in the highest frequency.

I think my hearing loss is a combination of overexposure to noise and as well as heredity. Both my parents, who are in now their early 90s, also had hearing loss and both of my grandfathers wore large hearing aids in their shirt pockets. I was fitted with Siemens Pure 700s, which I still wear.

I was shocked when I first wore them: I heard sounds that I had not heard in a long time, such as birds chirping and singing. I started wearing them several years earlier than my parents did. Nothing today replaces normal hearing. Even with hearing aids, I still have trouble at times with words and also distinguishing certain notes on the guitar if too much is going on, more so if I'm playing softly.

I enjoy getting together on occasion with a couple of friends to jam and play music. I prefer to play amplified acoustic or electric guitar with amps or monitors facing me. I don't enjoy playing guitar acoustically unless it has a microphone and I'm wearing headphones or I'm facing monitors. I like the sound to come at me from the front. I work with guitar amps occasionally--- I also have a few amplifiers and hearing aids are essential in getting the amps to sound right. I like to write songs and presently have a bunch in various stages of completion. I joined NSAI (Nashville Songwriters Association International) and want to become more involved with music.

I don't have any regrets or anger over my hearing loss, though I have, honestly, been somewhat disappointed at times. It's been one big inconvenience, to say the least. I get a little frustrated as most everyone but I always try to be positive and enjoy the moment each time I pick up the guitar or pen and paper to write a song or simply listening to music. I'm lucky to have musician friends who have good hearing that I can compare sounds with.

I have hopes, not so much for myself, but for others who have less hearing, that one day, the science, medical and technology fields will be able to restore hearing at least to some degree and maybe eliminate hearing aids and cochlear implants altogether. Who knows? Meanwhile, life goes on.

Sharon Campbell

Sharon Campbell—Amateur bass clarinetist
Pueblo, Colorado, USA

I was an Rh baby, where my mother's blood was attacking mine while in utero. I ended up with a moderate-severe cookie bite hearing loss, among other problems. I did not get my first pair of hearing aids until I was 7 years old. I think my parents didn't like my singing voice---perhaps because I'm functionally tone-deaf, so they had me take up clarinet when I was 10 years old. My hearing loss wasn't really a factor in my choice of musical instruments, but because I heard high frequencies normally and the hearing aids amplified them, I never found the sound of flutes attractive, and positively hated piccolos. Due to related coordination problems, I found it too difficult to play contra-alto and contrabass clarinet music. However, Mr. Richard Hayes moved me to bass clarinet in junior high school. I love the sound of the bass clarinet as well as the contra-alto (E-flat) and contra-bass (B-flat) clarinet. The music is far easier to play, and that has led me to become a lifetime musician.

I played clarinet while my friends played their guitars and sang popular songs in college (they wouldn't let me sing) and started on bass clarinet again in graduate school. Because my friends were saying something about not being able to sing the music if they changed their guitar key to match my Bb clarinet, I had to transpose. Up one note, add two sharps. The singer John Denver loved to start with three or, better, four sharps, so I got really good at playing those keys.

Playing with an ensemble of normally hearing musicians was (and still is) challenging since I mostly hear just what is immediately adjacent to me and nothing else. I tracked my part coordinating with what I hear around me, and kept an eagle eye on the conductor. (Apparently, this is a bit disconcerting to the conductors.) Over half of the information I received then and now is visual, and I am constantly looking for cues when I got lost. Music with changes in time signature and marked changes in dynamics and tempo made it easier.

However, fugues have always been a lost cause. I can usually play the first three or four measures; then, I get lost and will then join the rest of the band for that final whole note. If the conductor moved me to a different location, I could just as well be playing an entirely new set of music that I never heard or rehearsed, since the instruments around me that I used as markers changed. Playing in tune was and still is hard, too; if the dynamics of the piece is louder than mezzo piano, I could no longer hear my own horn. That has never bothered me; if I couldn't hear it when I played a wrong note, then it didn't matter. While I knew that sounded absurd, it worked for me emotionally. And besides, I've played in some very good ensembles and never been kicked out, so I couldn't have been too bad.

I finally got an Audex assistive listening device (ALD) in my thirties. I can put in a battery, put on the silhouettes or neckloop, adjust my hearing aids and add two microphones: one going down to the bell of my horn, and the other to the conductor's stand so I know what I am supposed to be playing. It was really freaky hearing myself play at first, but now I enjoy it. I like it when I play with just a few instruments and harmonize. Letters of the alphabet still don't usually compute, and I have trained my conductors to say "B as in baseball" or "one-four" so that I don't start playing at "D" and rehearsal number 40.

The other bonus is that I can hear the flutes, clarinets and oboes in the first row. I never could before getting the ALDs; so getting moved to a different location in the band isn't nearly as difficult. Of course, I have trained my conductors to not do that, either! Sometimes I'll put another splitter on the microphones so I can hear another instrument that I am doing a duet or trio with. And once I played in the pit band of "Cabaret," and I had a microphone on the piano/conductor, on the clarinet next to me, and one on my husband, so he could count off measures for me as I played.

The wired ALD systems are the most versatile, since I can use splitters to use as many or few microphones as I need, and I can even split the receiver, which I had to do with "Cabaret" since I had more microphones going than a single ALD had enough power for. I taped a second one to the music stand and used a reverse splitter to link them both to my silhouettes. Outside of music, I will use the splitter to share the ALD with another hard of hearing person. To do what I do with my wired system with an FM system would require a soundboard, which is expensive and a royal pain to hook up and transport. I can get extension cords of various lengths as I need them, and the only limit on functionality is my imagination.

Interestingly, playing with a small group, such as a jazz or Dixieland band does not require the use of the ALD because of new hearing aid technology. The digital technology is so superior to the analog hearing aids I started with many years ago that it is now a whole new world. My first analog hearing aids only amplified the speech frequencies, and mostly the high frequencies, at that. In fact, on hearing music with my first full-spectrum aids, I literally wept at the beauty of it. I didn't attempt much that was challenging hearing-wise when I was growing up.

Now I am enjoying new forays into music that I would never have dreamed of trying before. I play the soprano clarinet in German Band. Currently I am a member of eight (!) bands in the Pueblo, Colorado area, playing all sizes of clarinets as required. For the first time, I have been a member of pit bands for musicals, "Bye, Bye Birdie," "Big," and "Cabaret," playing bass and soprano clarinet. I also play the string bass part with swing and jazz bands on my contra-alto clarinet. I play bass clarinet with some clarinet choirs. I'm pretty much up for anything except music calling for more finger movement in too short a time to play accurately. Once, when we were playing "The Cowboys" by John Williams, I went through with MuseScore music writing software and rewrote it, eliminating virtually every triplet to make it manageable for my fingers. My conductors prefer that I do that rather than mangle what I can't play.

I am now the Southern Colorado Community Band Coordinator since I am pretty much a member of all the bands here, ensuring that nobody schedules a concert at the same time. There is too much musician overlap for that to work. I am also now helping to start and run community bands, and have run two successful Southern Colorado Community Music Festivals with a third in the planning stages.

But I still don't sing. I hear pitches much better now, and now even I can't stand the sound of my own singing.

Jennifer Castellano

Making Music with a Hearing Loss: Strategies and Stories

Jennifer Castellano—Pianist and composer
Thornwood, New York, USA

I was born both vision and hearing disabilities; however my impaired hearing was not officially diagnosed until I was eight years old. Strangely though, I didn't learn how to talk until I was three and a half years old. I think my family thought that I was just a late bloomer. After all, I didn't learn how to walk until I was two. They were also focused on helping me overcome my visual challenges. My hearing loss is what you call a cookie bite loss. That is, I can hear high and low frequencies better than the middle frequencies. Because I was able to hear high and low frequencies in both ears, it was thought that my hearing was okay.

I didn't decide to take piano lessons until an incident occurred at a friend's house when I was about seven years old. My childhood friend showed me a small electronic keyboard that had a series of buttons at the top. She pushed one button and soon I heard a simple melody with a drum accompaniment. I listened to it a couple times. Then she pushed another button, which produced the drum accompaniment alone. My fingers immediately jumped to the keyboard and I began playing the song exactly how I remembered it. My friend immediately jumped up and ran into the kitchen where her mother was. I followed to see what the excitement was all about. "Mom! Mom!" she cried, "She can play it!" I was shocked by her enthusiastic response. I had no idea what the big deal was. Wasn't that how everyone learned music? My friend's mother told me that I should take piano lessons.

I began studying piano when I was eight years old. I had my first piano lesson on March 1, 1990. It was a Thursday and I remember it fairly well. In a matter of minutes I had mastered where all the notes on the keyboard were (including sharps and flats). This was the first time I learned all their names. My teacher immediately noticed that I had a very good memory. A few weeks later she later discovered that I had perfect pitch.

A few months after my piano studies, I learned something about myself that would greatly influence my philosophy of hearing music. In May of 1990, I learned that I had a hearing loss and that I needed to wear hearing aids to help correct the problem. This came as a shock to me. I didn't know anyone my age who had a hearing impairment and who wore hearing aids. The only person I knew who had a hearing loss and wore hearing aids was my paternal grandmother, but her hearing loss was the result of aging. So when I was told that I needed a hearing aid, my first reaction was something like: "What? And skip middle age?"

It seemed like a paradox to be a musician with a hearing disability who had perfect pitch. On one hand, I was told that I had such a good musical ear, but on the other I was told that I was deaf as a door nail. Answering the telephone was a big fear of mine as a child because it was always difficult for me to hear the person on the other end.

It took me a while to accept my hearing loss for what it was but eventually I did accept it when I was 12 years old. Not only did I accept it, I never allowed it to prevent me from continuing my musical studies. In May 2004, I earned a Bachelor of Arts in Music at Manhattanville College where I concentrated in piano performance, and in May 2008, I completed a Master of Music at Purchase College where I concentrated in composition.

I didn't begin composing until I was in college and began studying music theory and composition with Mary Ann Joyce-Walter. When she began sharing some of original works with me, I began writing my own original works. Dr. Joyce was my very first teacher of composition who continues to be one of my biggest musical supporters and closest friends.

When writing music, I usually hear rhythm before melody. I do hear melodies but the first thing I take notice of is rhythm and meter. Rhythm is what makes my music tick. Not only can you hear rhythm but you can also feel it. When I was a choir singer back in college, our choral director had made a comment in reference to a rhythmic passage in one of our pieces: "I shouldn't hear any feet tapping. Rhythm is felt from within." I couldn't agree more.

My biggest challenges in music relate to both my vision and hearing. With my vision it was fairly obvious. I had difficulty reading printed music. My scores always had and continue to be enlarged to a readable size. Since 2005, I have been wearing a telescopic lens so I can read the score while sitting at a regular distance from the piano.

Aural challenges are a little less obvious. I have been wearing hearing aids since I was eight years old. While I can hear some sounds without them (like the high pitched calls of my two small parrots, Sunny and Nikki), I wear them all the time. They help make the sounds louder and clearer. I find the use of an FM system extremely helpful when playing chamber and ensemble music. I am in my church's handbell choir and our director always wears my FM transmitter at rehearsals so that I can better understand what she is saying.

In general, I can hear and recognize individual pitches and chords. However, when it comes to a piano's tone quality and touch, that is Greek to me. I could never tell if I was producing a nice sound or not. I could just hear loud and soft. I would spend a long time trying to figure out if the phrase "moved" in the right way or if the melody could be heard above the accompaniment. I never knew how the balance between the hands was. When I was in college, a lot of my jury comments stated that I produced a harsh tone. This always confused me. What did a harsh tone sound like compared a nice one? Even today I sometimes find it hard to tell the difference when I listen to other pianists play.

My senses were only able to do so much for me. It wasn't until I started my piano studies with Flora Kuan that things started to make more sense. I don't know if anyone ever told her that her teaching methods are a gift to piano students with hearing loss, but I would have to say this statement holds true. Since we began working together, I now play with more ease and confidence.

Dr. Kuan would not describe how a passage should sound by only using aural or visual words. She would often use words that related to touch and feeling. "It should feel gummy and sticky." she would say in reference to a legato passage. With regard to tone quality she would say something like: "You cannot produce a nice sound when your hand is hard. It has to be soft. The wrist cannot be tight. It has to be loose." Or when referring to a passage that required a strong yet mellow tone she would say something like: "You have to cushion the sound. Move your wrists down slowly but firmly." Now I was starting to get it. I might have not been able to hear an extreme difference but I could feel it and that is how I knew if I were producing the right kind of sound.

I truly learned the real art of listening. It goes far beyond the human ear. Over time, I learned to pay attention to how sound traveled through parts of my body: my finger tips, hands, wrists, arms and even my shoulders and back.

One of the most memorable things that Dr. Kuan ever said to me was that "Music is for everybody." It was amazing to hear something like that come from an accomplished musician, but I agree with her. Music is not about being the best but about giving your best. It isn't about how much ability you have, but how you use your ability. This brings to mind to the quotation by American author, educator and clergyman, Henry Van Dyke, who once said: "Use what talents you possess: the woods would be very silent if no birds sang there except those that sang best."

"To play a wrong note is insignificant. To play without passion is inexcusable."

Ludwig Van Beethoven, German composer

Kathy Castellucci

Kathy Castellucci—Singer
Orlando, Florida, USA

I grew up in a very musical family, as my father was a music teacher and I was exposed to a lot of music growing up. I played flute and piccolo in middle and high school. At the age of 16 I started singing in a choir and a few a cappella groups. Singing in these vocal groups helped me to realize that I really loved to sing and wanted to become a professional singer. I studied voice performance in college, and then became a professional singer at Disney World and Universal Studios in Orlando. I loved my life and my job.

Fast forward to about 15 years later when some embarrassing events started happening. I could not stay on pitch and music became confusing. I started asking people to repeat themselves. I would turn around to a room full of co-workers laughing because they called my name several times and I did not respond. I saw people making faces in the audience . . . and not the good kind. I was asked at work to have my hearing tested and that's when the initial shock came. I was rapidly losing my hearing and it was also causing my pitch perception to be distorted.

The next 6 years became the most challenging, heartbreaking and embarrassing years I've ever experienced. My career started taking a nosedive, but I was determined to not let go of the one thing I loved to do. The only problem was that it wasn't making me happy any more; it was causing me emotional pain.

As my hearing continued to deteriorate, I started to shut down even in social situations. I went through every test imaginable, but there is still no answer as to why I was quickly losing my hearing. I started wearing hearing aids, which is a difficult transition for anyone.

It was discouraging, confusing to my brain, and caused some intense headaches. In-ear monitors helped somewhat but they weren't correcting my frequency loss so my pitch was still off and everything still sounded muffled. I had the unlucky task of testing all of this on stage in front of thousands of people every day trying to sing my heart out and failing miserably. It was devastating.

The people I worked for stuck with me, for a time. But slowly those people dropped off one by one. I was not considered a good singer anymore; I was more of a liability.

I was criticized plenty by those who did not know of my struggle, and even some that did. I wanted to enjoy performing alongside my friends and co-workers, but I couldn't anymore. I felt like an outcast among them. My career fell behind as theirs all moved forward. I stopped listening to music almost altogether unless I had to for work, and I shed a lot of tears over not knowing who I was anymore.

It was a difficult thing to go through but luckily there is an upswing to this story. I traveled this bumpy road alongside some people who still believed in me and did not give up on me. And thankfully, I did not give up on myself.

I chased my hearing loss around every corner with the latest technology, always looking for workable solutions. My audiologist and I have turned this whole process into an experiment which has truly kept me going. Since the in-ear monitors were not helping my pitch, I eventually had to abandon them once better technology was offered.

Recently, I started using Resound Linx2 hearing aids that allow me to have Bluetooth control over everything I hear. The hearing aids are preset to correct my exact frequency losses and then on top of that they pair with the Apple iOS devices such as iPhone and are controlled with an app. The reason they help me so much as a singer is I have volume, bass and treble controls that I can change right on the app.

These allow me to control the stage volume and bass/treble frequencies as needed to have a better understanding of pitch reference. I recently got an Apple Watch so now I wear that on stage and I can control those settings right from my wrist. What an amazing tool this is for a musician, but also for anyone who struggles with hearing loss.

It has helped me to improve my pitch while giving me back my confidence and my enjoyment of singing.

During those years of musical turmoil, I stayed determined. I immersed myself into other facets of my career. While working through my challenges on stage, I began utilizing my knowledge of the business behind the scenes for several entertainment companies. I have since started my own company and with the help of technology, I now have a wonderful career on and off stage.

This journey has given me a completely different perspective on life that I am truly grateful for. I pushed through and fought for what I loved. I could never take anything for granted again. It's a beautiful place to be and I'm thankful for all of those people that have seen me through it. Who knows what the future will bring? I definitely have no idea, but I'm certainly not scared. I'm excited to see what's next. And I know now that I'm ready for anything.

Shih-wen Angela Chen

Shih-wen Angela Chen—Amateur pianist and singer
Taipei, Taiwan

I was born in a loving and happy family in Taiwan. When I was three, my mother became aware of my unusual hearing situation, and that's when I was diagnosed with a mild hearing loss in my right ear and a profound hearing loss in my left ear. I was blessed that while my right ear's hearing kept deteriorating to severe level through the years, I still lived a joyful childhood without feeling limited by my hearing loss.

I started piano lessons at the age of six and studied it for seven years. I happily fell into the world of music and enjoyed the beautiful moments of playing the piano. When I became eleven years old, the hearing in my right ear suddenly deteriorated from mild to a moderate level. Daily life became difficult. I started wearing hearing aids and using an FM system at school. With my hearing aids, my hearing loss did not impose much negative impact on me when playing the piano, because I could always rely on the music score and match the piano keys to notes in my brain. However, when listening to music without a score for reference, I could only perceive a rough melodic contour, and could not recognize or repeat the melody precisely. Different instruments in a symphony sounded like a mess to me, and I could barely recognize the harmonies. If I did not have access to the music score, many different music pieces would sound indistinguishable – it's like you're watching a movie in a foreign language without subtitles, and everything buzzes in a similarly messy tone. Needless to say, I lost my ability to sing in tune; I couldn't tell if I was on or off pitch and began to lose confidence in my ability to sing. As a result, I felt insecure when singing. I needed extra practice with the piano and assistance from my family when preparing for music class in school.

Music still appealed to me so much, yet I had to do more to become intimately aware of aural music. My strategies as a teenager were to purchase a large quantity of sheet music and play them on the piano or read them while listening to music. I loved to sing karaoke with friends but I would never sing alone. I would study music scores before attending instrumental music concerts. I would dance with friends but I would also memorize the music and practice counting the beats beforehand.

While attending college at National Taiwan University, a lot of my friends participated in an amateur mixed chorus called the Ching-Yun Chorus. I had never thought about joining a chorus, but my friends gave me some encouraging information about this chorus. I attended one of their concerts and was shocked – I didn't even know that the human voice could produce so many varied sounds, and when they sang with true joy, I could feel it even though I had no access to the score beforehand. The more I heard from my friends and the chorus concerts, the more I become fascinated by choral music. It was such an amazing world there! I had no experience in singing in a chorus, but I was fortunate that senior singers in the Chorus maintained a positive attitude and suggested me to try singing instead of putting limits on myself. They enrolled a lot of new, inexperienced singers every year, and they did not require perfect diction from novice singers. They welcomed me warmly and assigned a very capable singer to sit beside me to correct my pitch and teach me how to sing. I greatly appreciated what they did, and I was so glad that I could become an alto singer. (I was assigned to sing in the alto part because I would sing out of tune more often when singing in a higher register.)

My right ear had a severe hearing loss then. At first, the four vocal parts sounded like they were in disarray. I couldn't even hear my own voice, let alone tell if my pitch matched the singer sitting next to me. I was frustrated, but I found that after several months' practice, I could sing better. I found myself trying to remember the feeling of my whole body when I was told that I was singing in tune. That sometimes worked – I experimented again and again during each practice. I tried to develop an inner system that related my throat's vibration and my body's feeling to the pitch I sang. And then I relied on the singers sitting around me to tell me if I should sing higher or lower to train this system.

Meanwhile, my hearing continued to be trained a lot as well. I surprisingly found that even though my hearing was impaired, it could still be trained. Through long weekly practices, I could hear myself, and then I could gradually recognize melodies from different vocal parts. Harmonies no longer sounded like an entangled muddle. This development greatly encouraged me. After several years in the chorus, I could now sing on pitch steadily after some practices of feeling my throat vibrating and hearing my neighbor. I could even follow my neighbor's or accompanying instrument's pitch and correct myself. I now looked forward to performing in public more and more. I enjoyed the beauty of choral music and the moments when we singers were all inspired by the vocal harmonies surrounding us.

Three years ago, I suddenly lost what remained of my hearing and underwent cochlear implant. After I recovered from the surgery and received a cochlear implant in my right ear, I returned to my chorus – and found things became easier. The details that I had lost in music now all reappeared. That was super exciting. I now need to train myself and develop a new singing system based on my new bionic hearing.

Last year, I had my left ear implanted as well. This is the first time in my entire life that I am finally able to hear in stereo. Choral concerts now sounded entirely different, reinvigorated my soul, and left me teary-eyed – oh the beauty of aural music thrilled me. I deeply cherish the newfound ability to understand aural music which my two cochlear implants have allowed me to do.

I wish to thank to my family and everyone else who has helped me on my musical journey thus far. And I look forward to my new life singing with bilateral cochlear implants.

Wendy Cheng

Wendy Cheng—Viola and voice student
Gaithersburg, Maryland, USA

Since I was 9 years old, hearing loss has impacted my life significantly. I am told I was born with normal hearing, yet I have no memory of what it was like to hear with two normally functioning ears.

The hearing loss was discovered during a routine school screening when I was in the third grade. My parents think the loss is the result of ototoxic medications administered to me when I was 2 years old. At the time of diagnosis, my right ear was found to have a profound hearing loss and my left ear had a mild to moderate loss. Over the years, the left ear slowly deteriorated, and then settled down at 70 dB across all frequency ranges. I wore a Phonic Ear behind-the-ear hearing aid in my left ear for many years.

I think I've always had an affinity for music, even when I was a baby. My mother noted that I enjoyed being lulled to sleep with radio music. Mom had all three girls in our family study classical piano, so I had piano lessons from the age of 7 to 15. Starting in high school, I fell in love with the sound of the violin but no one in my family gave me, a person with a severe hearing loss, much chance of success with this instrument, since the intonation requirements for this instrument is so much higher than the piano. Nevertheless the desire to play the violin and to call this instrument my own continued to tug at my heart. To make a long story short, I finally began violin lessons at the age of 19 as a college sophomore, and haven't stopped ever since. I've participated in string quartets, string orchestra and full orchestra workshops.

I've been very blessed to have good violin and viola instructors who found ways to work around my significant hearing loss. Some of them taught me to relax my fingers around the fingerboard so that I could feel the strong vibration on a few of the notes on the fingerboard. I learned to listen for the sympathetic ringing tones anytime I played a note that was an octave of the open strings (G, D, A, E). I taught myself to use an electronic tuner to help me learn the distance between the notes when shifting into higher. I used black duct tape on the fingerboard to mark the few notes that I just could not hear well enough to place my fingers in the right location.

I suffered a viral infection and lost the remainder of my hearing when I was 32 years old. I decided to get a cochlear implant and in January 1997 received a Clarion 1.2 implant in my right ear. Today, I am the proud recipient of bilateral Harmony cochlear implants from Advanced Bionics. Due to these implants, I have been able gain some idea of what it is like to have bilateral hearing.

Within a year of receiving my first cochlear implant, I began easing myself back into violin playing. It was slow going. Cochlear implants at that time were mostly designed for speech perception and not for music enjoyment, much less for music performance. Yet, I know month after month, I was able to begin distinguishing when notes on sheet music sounded different from one another. I enjoyed how I could play music even though the auditory quality was only a fair approximation of how I heard through hearing aids.

In 2002, I ran into a new problem----- my cochlear implant wasn't helping me to distinguish notes at very high frequencies; every note on the violin E string above third position sounded the same. I felt like I had reached a roadblock in becoming the best string player I could be since I could not play in the higher positions on the violin. With some trepidation, I decided to switch to viola. Learning any bowed string instrument lower than the viola was out of the question because my implant also had problems discriminating notes in the lower ranges of the piano. The viola seemed to be a good compromise and I do enjoy learning to play the Bach cello suite transcribed for the viola.

Since receiving a second implant in my left ear in 2008, I have been able to do several things I could not do before. First, I can now hear the resonance on the viola more clearly in fifth position on the viola A string. Secondly, not only did I take up playing handbells and handchimes, I am now leading a handchime ensemble at the federal agency where I work. Lastly, I am now able to sing in tune with the piano and am also taking voice lessons.

There are several strategies I have used over the years to integrate my hearing loss into my musical studies. The first and foremost is using an assistive listening device (ALD). The idea is to have the music teacher or the conductor wear the transmitter unit while I wear the receiver unit. This resolves the thorny issue of needing to lip-read the teacher while getting instructions on playing an instrument (and oftentimes you're expected to be looking at the instrument instead of the teacher's face).

So far I have found Comtek's AT-216 FM system and Etymotic Research's Companion Mic system to work the best in my musical lessons. I can plug the Comtek system's transmitter into the digital piano I have so I get to hear all the notes pretty well. I use the Companion Mic system when playing string quartets or participating in small ensembles at a camp for adult string players. I have the violinists in the group wear the Companion Mic transmitters and this really helps in ensuring I can hear the other players and not get lost as often as before. I also use the Companion Mic system during my voice lessons, when I wear the receiver and place one transmitter unit on the piano. My voice teacher wears a transmitter too.

Some other strategies I use involve ways to get around the high intonation requirements of learning to play an unfretted bowed string instrument, especially since my viola does not give strong vibrations and not all notes have ringing tones to help me determine whether I am playing in tune or not. These days I use the Tunable app on my iPhone to help me discern in a visual way how much (or how little) I am in tune, and to assist in developing my visual and spatial memory. I use a visual metronome app so that I don't need to depend on aural cues alone to help me develop the rhythmic timing needed to play well.

Having spent the last twenty years developing my skills as an amateur string player, I am eager to see how the next twenty years unfold. Hopefully I will be able to fulfill a life-long dream of obtaining a music degree in the next few years.

Eva Costa

Eva Costa—Recorderist and music teacher
Faro, Portugal

I was born with impaired hearing. When I was 2 and half years old, my adenoids were removed. After that surgery, I was able to hear better but I still had a mild hearing loss in both ears.

When I reached my 6th birthday, I started attending recorder classes. I chose this instrument because my brother was going to recorder classes and if he was going I had to go, too. I also started taking piano lessons when I was 9 years old. However, after 5 years of playing both instruments, I finally decided that the recorder was my instrument of choice. I just liked the sound of the recorder more and I wanted to continue with my studies to master this instrument.

I have two Bachelor's degrees in music; the first degree is in teaching music (music education) and the second one is in early music performance with a focus on the recorder. At this moment, I'm finishing up my Master's degree in teaching recorder. It has been very hard to play having a hearing impairment, but I always did the best that I could. I never gave up and I finished my two undergraduate degrees in 2005 and 2011. In fact, most of my teachers didn't even know that I have a hearing loss and evaluated me just like a music student with normal hearing. I'm proud of completing two music degrees through my own efforts alone.

The biggest challenge in making music with a hearing disability is achieving good intonation. I play an instrument which requires having great sensitivity to air vibrations to achieve good intonation. When you have hearing loss, this capability is weak and most of the time trying to tune your instrument does not produce accurate results.

Before I received my first middle ear implant in 2014, I always had to ask to the violinist to play a long A note or the harpsichordist to play an arpeggio. I used the A note as a reference in my head. Now, with this middle ear implant, I can now hear other instruments better and it also helps me tune my recorder more accurately and play solo works with better intonation.

I adapted to my condition as a girl with hearing loss; I always tried to do my best, and never gave up. My goal in life is to always do better today than I did yesterday.

Nanette Florian

Nanette Florian—Pianist, bassist and songwriter
Rockville, Connecticut, USA

All the signs were in front of my family and myself. I was slowly losing my hearing but no one acknowledged this. My father wore big, powerful hearing aids, but claimed it all came from the bombs in the war. My uncles, my grandfathers, everyone in my family had hearing aids; but when the school nurse told me in second grade that my hearing was down a bit, nobody made a big deal. Because hearing loss was seen as normal in my family, no one recognized that the pattern was repeating itself with the next generation.

A painting of Beethoven hung on the wall behind our family piano---this is the painting where he is taking a break from his writing and looking sternly down. My father shipped it home from Italy during the war. There I sat year after year, playing the piano and singing away while Beethoven looked on, perhaps knowing the day would come when I'd have to give it up and join him. There were two sure components of my life: musical abilities and this sneaky emerging deafness . . . "deafinitely" an awkward combination!

It was wonderful while the music lasted. Singing songs felt like flying and gave me an emotional high. Musical theater was my favorite activity and I sang and acted in every local production I could find as a teenager. After graduating from high school, I joined up with my brother, William who is also musical. We bought a motor home and we sang our way across the country as a musical duo. William was hell-bent on us becoming music stars.

We made our way to California where we auditioned for the New Christy Minstrels, a famous group from the 1960s that continued to tour and hire new musicians. They told us not to bother but we barged into their office anyways, with William lugging up his guitar and me my standup bass. We got in and I was the first female bass player for the Christies, and possibly the youngest to join at age 19. Out first concert with the New Christy Minstrels was at the California State Fair after just a few rehearsals. I'm not sure I had all the songs "down" that afternoon, but I sure had fun acting like I did!

After returning to the East Coast I played the piano and sang at every venue possible in Connecticut, Atlantic City in New Jersey and in Florida. I had taught myself to play by "ear." I played in piano bars, nightclubs, restaurants, and parties and wherever people would listen to my renditions of Billie Holiday, Carole King, show tunes, and everything in between. I'm grateful I had 40 years of hearing beautifully rendered aural music. Music was who I was!

Even though I wore small "in-the-ear" hearing aids as a young adult, I continued to play and sing. The hearing aids I wore became bigger and bigger in size as my hearing loss progressed. However, I never dreamed that one day I wouldn't be able to even recognize the songs the church choir I directed was singing. I was teaching someone a part I wrote for him to sing and he had this puzzled expression on his face. That's when it hit me. "What? I'm off key?" He nodded. I used to have perfect pitch. The day I realized I was singing off key in church was the day my singing career was over. My hearing loss had hit rock bottom.

I finally underwent cochlear implant surgery. The cochlear implant processor brought conversation back into my life. I could talk on the telephone again. I didn't have to be centered in front of someone to "try" to read his or her lips. The very night after they turned on the processor (a month after surgery) I could hear what my husband was saying on the telephone in the next room!! I proceeded to jump up and down and scream, "I can HEAR YOU!" They said I caught on fast possibly because my musical training probably helped me to understand the intonation found in spoken language.

Hurray, I could join the world again! The cochlear implant processor allows me to hear people talking but music is very difficult to hear! I can only hear what the processor allows me to hear (it has an electronic-like quality) and through the processor, music sounds off-key! It sounds like the song is underwater. This makes the singer and the instruments sound like they're in different keys. Although it's a lot harder to hear now, I still play the piano, because I remember where my fingers should be, and the piano is always in tune, even though I don't hear it that way.

Having that big, musical void in my life was depressing. Not only could I not sing and perform, it was difficult to even listen to music. The only songs I hear now are the ones I knew before I went deaf. My brain remembers them and I can follow along. I haven't heard any new songs since maybe 1990. If "oldies" are playing on the radio, I will ask whoever is with me "What song is this?" I'll listen closely, and if I know it, my memory will take over and I'll hear pretty clearly. What I do hear when music is playing is, rhythm, phrasing, and lyrics, but the melody comes out sounding like rap music.

Beethoven composed some of his memorable symphonies after he lost his hearing. How did he do this? Well, I know, because it's how I write songs now--- It's all in my head. Writing songs is how I can be a musician again. My songs are the new ones I can hear . . . I hear them because they started in my mind. Now I make demo recordings in my home studio of the songs I write (I play the piano, someone else sings, and, then, with a group of talented musicians, we record them in a professional studio. I feel musical again! Three of my songs are being represented by Music of the Sea Publishing in Chicago.

After being passed around the family for many years, that painting of Beethoven has a prominent place in my living room once again over the piano: I feel his presence, he is still watching, taking notes and perhaps thinking "Go girl!"

I made a music video recently with my song: "Beethoven and me". You can watch it on my website, www.nanetteflorian.com.

Mischa Goelke

Mischa Goelke—Guitarist and guitar teacher
Founder & Project Leader of "Limitations are Relative"
Hamburg, Germany

When I was about 16 years old, I heard blues-rock guitarist
Stevie Ray Vaughn perform and was completely overcome by
the experience. I was deeply drawn to his music and felt an
irresistible urge to start playing the guitar. The fact that I had
been born with a severe-to-profound hearing loss was not going
to stop me.

The causes of my borderline inner-and-middle-ear deafness
are not completely understood. Either I was deprived briefly of
oxygen at birth or my mother took ototoxic medications when she
was pregnant. In any case, I received my first hearing aid when I
was three years old. I still vividly remember running through the
store after my first hearing aid fitting, tapping against everything
with a wooden spoon and being enthralled by the sounds.

With hearing aids I hear about 60% of total volume, but I
am missing many sounds, particularly those in the mid and high
frequency ranges. For me, hearing and understanding are two different things. I hear speech and music in general as a sonic mush.
The clarity of what I hear vacillates constantly. Over and over
again, I experience moments when I can't understand a thing followed by other times when I hear everything clearly....

Widespread beliefs such as "due to a hearing impairment one
cannot make music," or "I have no talent to sing," or "You're
too old to start something new," are limiting thought patterns by
which we are conditioned.

For 5 years I gave music lessons to deaf as well as hearing
students. Although seemingly paradoxical, giving "normal" music lessons to the hearing impaired is possible when we ignore the
supposed limitations. In one example, a woman in her 50s took
guitar lessons for the first time. She wanted to experience music
despite always having been told she would not be unable to hear
if she played the notes correctly. We played a tune and it became
clear that she had wonderful tone perception as well as a talent

for phrasing—her phrase was better probably than most of my normally hearing students.

One of our biggest mistakes is projecting on deaf and hard of hearing people the "normal" processes in making music and in living life in general. Some individuals with "normal" hearing cannot distinguish between two tones. Some individuals with hearing loss can train their hearing to understand music.

During many phases of my life, I had doubted my own abilities. When I focused on my supposed disabilities I often became a victim of my own doubts. We are all differently "abled....", but the real barriers are mental barriers, and not necessarily sensory barriers. With passion, discipline, and persistence, we can do almost anything.

"Music is the arithmetic of sound as optics is the geometry of light."

Claude Debussy, French composer

Angela Hill

Angela Hill—Pianist
Norfolk, Virginia, USA

I was diagnosed with a hearing loss at the age of 6, initially wearing one hearing aid, then hearing aids in both ears. My hearing loss was moderate, progressing bilaterally into the severe/profound to profound range.

Despite having a moderate hearing loss as a child, I was still able to enjoy music, particularly the piano. I started playing the piano at the age of 6. Music had such an impact on my life that I decided early on that I wanted to somehow make a career in music. By high school, I began giving private piano lessons, which continued until around year 1991. In college, I majored in music education, with emphasis on the piano and graduated cum laude in 1988.

It was not until the end of high school that I noticed worsening hearing, but I felt it could be helped with stronger hearing aids. By my junior year in college, it was obvious that something was wrong but I persevered, even continuing through student teaching at three public schools. Eventually, I had to give up teaching music as a career.

After nearly a 20-year hiatus, I underwent cochlear implant surgery in my right ear and gradually re-introduced my bionic ear to the piano. What joy it was to be back at the piano bench! For over three years, I was bi-modal, utilizing a hearing aid in the left ear and cochlear implant in the right ear. I had the opportunity to play at church, events, and conferences. The mapping skills and the expertise of my cochlear implant audiologist is what allowed me to maximize my ability to play the piano once again.

In December 2015, I underwent cochlear implant surgery in my left ear. I have been activated for the last three weeks and it is an interesting adjustment experience. Playing piano with a second bionic ear is almost identical as if I was playing bi-modal, but right now I do not perceive the bass notes as I have been able to do so while bi-modal (when listening to music from the radio or the television). However, my surgeon and audiologist feel that I will be able to perceive that same level of bass or close to it in good time. So it's a continuing process of having my brain adjust to the new sounds coming from both bionic ears. The future looks bright as I continue on my musical journey as a pianist with bilateral cochlear implants.

Matthew Mack

Matthew Mack—Cellist
Melbourne, Australia

I was born in 1989 in Sydney, Australia with a congenital hearing loss inherited from my mother's side of the family. My family was vaguely aware that I was showing a few symptoms of hearing loss from birth to toddlerhood. However, when I was two years old, I happened to be standing next to a telephone when it rang. When I did not respond to the ringing of the phone, my mother rushed me to the pediatrician's office.

I have a profound hearing loss in my right ear and a mild-severe loss in my left ear, which is now fitted with a behind-the-ear hearing aid. When I was five years old, my parents felt that learning a musical instrument would be an excellent way to expand my awareness of sound. At that time the only instruments taught at my primary school were violin and cello, and the latter seemed to be the appropriate option given my high-frequency hearing loss.

I've certainly given my audiologists a hard time in fine-tuning the music-specific program on these hearing aids, mainly due to the difficulty in describing differences in the subtle nuances in music. In high school I was using a Siemens Music Pro, then a Siemens Prisma, and now a Siemens Micon – all of which I've adjusted to and have been very happy with, especially with the progressive improvement in technology and capabilities.

In terms of assistive listening devices, while I've not explicitly used any of them for music, the Phonak Smartlink SX was a microphone that my teachers and lecturers could wear which transmits the audio to an attachment on my hearing aid, allowing me to hear them clearly over a short distance.

This has now been upgraded to the Roger Pen, a much more inconspicuous device which performs the same functions and more.

I have little memory of my hearing loss being a problem in my earlier years of cello playing, but never did I feel that I was behind my peers. It wasn't until after I was accepted into the University of Melbourne to study music that I began to face hearing-related obstacles.

Aural tests were a mandatory component of my music study, involving transcription of rhythms and melodies. I was also required to identify scales and chords by ear, as well as being able to sing and clap simple passages while conducting and counting respectively. In my experience, the university's staff and the disability liaison unit have always been receptive to my needs. Special arrangements for my aural tests involved conducting the tests in a room with just the examiner and myself, where I would be seated close to the source of the sound (the piano that the examiner plays on, or the speakers if the sound was produced from a recording). The aim of such arrangements is to ensure that there is minimal noise (from the environment or presence of other students) that could interrupt or distort the sound I was required to listen to.

Playing in orchestras was problematic as I am unable to distinguish the sound of my own instrument from others. As a result it was difficult to tell if I was in tune with the rest of the orchestra, and even with arrangements made to have myself seated next to a more experienced cellist to provide feedback when necessary, the overall anxiety combined with the fact that I've always felt alone within an orchestra (presumably as a byproduct of my introversion and depression), ended up being a major factor dissuading me from participating in large ensembles.

Small ensembles (e.g. chamber ensembles) are more manageable due to having fewer instruments to keep track of. I've found myself relying on studying the score and memorizing my colleagues' parts (as opposed to picking things up by ear) in order to ensure that I am in time with them.

A recent attempt at participating in a supporting band for local pop singers proved to be difficult as my colleagues and the singers were not reliant on sheet music, but a chord progression sheet and a sheet of lyrics. As my colleagues improvised and performed from memory, I didn't have a sufficient visual reference to fall back upon if I got lost mid-performance.

My understanding of my hearing loss' impact on my music ability is further compounded by the fact that I possess absolute pitch (the ability to name a note without a reference), since it implies that I perceive music differently to those with relative pitch. Never mind the obvious fact that my hearing loss in itself also impacts on my music perception! Nevertheless I am thankful that I am able to appreciate music on some level.

Nowadays I enjoy teaching privately, as the one-on-one interaction avoids any potential communication issues caused by extraneous noise. I've also taken pleasure in creating and playing arrangements of music that I enjoy listening to – the only major roadblock is my inability to transcribe recordings consisting of more than a single melody, in which I either find other arrangements or transcriptions and rearrange them as necessary, or ask someone to transcribe the passages that I cannot.

My main goal for cello playing in the near future is to release recordings and arrangements on YouTube. My main inspiration is ThePianoGuys, although 2Cellos definitely do deserve a mention for their ingenuity.

It should be made clear that the majority of my music experiences involve classical music, which has an extremely high barrier for professional entry. It is important to realize that hard of hearing musicians will have to work harder than those with normal hearing, and I myself cannot recommend a professional career in classical music performance for individuals with significant hearing loss. However, given how much enjoyment and wonder music brings to the masses, everyone, hard-of-hearing or not, is certainly encouraged to pick up a musical instrument.

Charles Mokotoff

(photo by C. Mokotoff)

Charles Mokotoff—Classical guitarist
Potomac, Maryland, USA

I experienced a sudden onset of hearing loss in both ears at 15 years of age. It left me with a severe-to-profound loss, which thankfully has not worsened significantly over the years. I had already been playing guitar in some local rock groups with friends and decided to continue playing despite the hearing loss. When I got to college I met someone playing classical guitar, and was completely hooked. I was totally awed by it. I picked up a classical guitar somewhere and just kept on working at it with the help of several very good and understanding teachers.

Besides the beguiling beauty of the guitar music, the other thing that really attracted me to the guitar was that it is predominantly a solo instrument. I did not have to worry about communicating with other members of a band or ensemble. I graduated cum laude from Syracuse University with a bachelor's degree in music, concentrating on classical guitar and then went on to Ithaca College, where I received a master's degree in the same field. I was immediately hired to teach in the music department at Ithaca and began a performance career that went on for about 15 years.

I made my Carnegie Hall debut in 1987 and in addition to performances on the East coast, played several concert tours in the Far East, including stops in Singapore, the Philippines and Hong Kong. Communicating overseas with many for whom English was not their first language was a particular challenge. Despite all the difficulties I overcame, in 1992 I decided to stop playing. It seemed I had reached as far as I could go, and had began to wonder what it would be like to live life where I didn't feel my hearing loss would be seen as something peculiar. Along the way I studied Information Technology, got several jobs in this field, married a deaf woman, had two beautiful children, got divorced and started to play again.

When I picked up the guitar in 2006, I was wearing digital hearing aids: the sound was far different than I recalled from my old analog days. Without a doubt, the most challenging aspect of this for me was trying to discover what the baseline is for me.

What does the guitar really sound like? How is my tone compared to other players? Is my perception of what is coming out of the instrument similar to what hearing audience members perceive? I've never really been able to answer these questions; it is an issue I have struggled with for a while and am beginning to accept by recording and studying and getting the opinion of people I trust. If I use a hearing aid music program that equalizes sounds that would otherwise seem strident to me, I am concerned I will become lazy since the cause of the discord could be my playing, not the hearing aid. But if I simply have a music program that corrects my loss, certain notes, in the frequencies in which I have the most severe loss, sound unbearable. However, with experience I have begun to make progress in remediating what comes out of my guitar with my own aural perception.

Since I am primarily a soloist, communicating with others is rarely an issue. But I do enjoy chamber music occasionally and am painfully aware that my music program doesn't help me enough with speech discrimination. I either switch back and forth, or just have to focus more on any conversations with my playing partners. Playing music with hearing aids in conversation mode is not an option.

My advice to anyone grappling with these issues is to have a very patient audiologist and try out as many types of technology as possible. Despite being quite open about my hearing loss, I still try to keep a low profile so have not experimented with assistive listening devices, which might serve others with different types of hearing loss much better than for me.

"You must play for the love of music. Perfect technique is not as important as making music from the heart."

Mstislav Rostropovich, Russian cellist

Dawn Mollenkopf

Dawn Mollenkopf—Amateur singer, violinist and pianist
Kearney, Nebraska, USA

I was born with a moderately-severe-to-moderate conductive loss due to Branchio-Oto-Renal Syndrome and, as early as I can remember, I was drawn to music. My journey into the world of musical instruments began with my climbing up onto the bench of my mom's electric keyboard one morning when I was four, and waking my parents up with "Mary Had A Little Lamb." However, my parents could not afford lessons until I was in third grade when someone gave us their piano. I found the piano easy to learn because much of the sound was in my hearing range and the keys provided a visual framework for sight-reading. My only real difficulty was with pedaling which I simply memorized for each song. I took lessons for several years, became a strong sight-reader, and by high school I played advanced pieces.

In eighth grade, I fell in love with the violin when a travelling orchestra came to our town. It was my first concert and I was fascinated by the stringed instruments. On the way home, I told my mom, "I want to play the violin." My mom first tried to discourage me because she thought I was too old to learn, but she saw that I was insistent so she bought a violin and signed me up for lessons.

I struggled at first because my violin teacher had me play by ear, which I could not do. So my mom found another teacher who let me sight read. Although the violin was more difficult to play than the piano, I found memorizing hand positions and developing a sense of touch for the fingering worked well. Bowing was a matter of mastering weight, speed, and control. The violin frequencies also fit well in my hearing range. I soon joined the youth orchestra my violin teacher started and she sat me in the front where I could hear, so I was able to perform well.

I started out as a music major in college but the music faculty was unsupportive and discouraged my attempts, so I changed my major. However, because voice lessons were required for music majors, I took a year of voice, which allowed me to explore vocal music. I struggled with solo work because I could not hear the piano accompaniment enough to sing with it, but I could follow along in a choir if someone with my part sang in my left ear.

After college, I entered the workforce, got involved with other activities, and music got shifted to the side, although I still played my instruments for personal enjoyment. Then I moved to a town with a small synagogue that had no rabbi, and I was asked to fill in as their soloist musician. Since they followed the oral tradition, all singing was unaccompanied. This freed me to sing and develop my voice as a soloist while leading many of the services.

When I started my doctorate, music again went on hold. After I graduated and got my current professor position, I began to experiment again with music. However, by now my hearing had dropped significantly and I had a severe to profound mixed loss, with an 80-decibel loss, flat line, in my left ear, and a 90- to 110-decibel loss in my right. My hearing aids were powerful enough to allow me to hear quality speech out of my left ear and good localization on my right but the feedback mechanism created whistling and distortion when I played an instrument or sang. Also, because my hearing had changed so dramatically I was feeling insecure when singing and was not sure how to correct my voice if things didn't sound or feel right.

As the lay leader in my Jewish community I was frequently called on to sing; therefore, I decided to address vocal issues first before working again with the piano or violin. So I joined the Association of Adult Musicians with Hearing Loss (AAMHL), which provided useful resources and connected me with people who had similar challenges.

I started voice lessons to retrain my ears to compensate for my new hearing levels, and I bought an Etymotic Companion Mic system, a personal FM system that allows for three speakers and one receiver. I took my Companion Mic system with me to voice lessons and used the transmitters for my teacher and one for the piano.

I am now in my fifth year of voice lessons. My teacher is very supportive and capitalizes on my sense of feel, sight, and residual hearing. I find voice my hardest instrument because it's the one I cannot see. However, I can usually match pitch well and have good tonal memory between measures, which helps me handle entrances throughout a song. To sing foreign languages, I use an online International Phonetic Alphabet interactive chart, which allows me to both hear a vowel or consonant and see a description of how it is formed. I get further coaching from my voice teacher on how to form those sounds. Singing with an accompaniment is still very difficult for me; however, my teacher has been able to select some songs where the accompaniment is easier to distinguish. I recently located a local pianist willing to practice with my voice teacher and me, and at the AAMHL conference in May 2015, I was able to perform two songs with accompaniment from another AAMHL member during the amateur hour.

My journey with music continues. This year, I plan to continue experimenting with singing opportunities involving an accompanist to refine this skill and in about a year, I would like start lessons back up for piano and violin. I continue to investigate newer hearing aids and listening devices as these options become available. I do not know how my musical journey will continue to evolve. However, I do know that music will always be an important part of my life.

Renee Blue O'Connell

Renee Blue O'Connell—Singer, songwriter, guitarist and music practitioner
Charlottesville, Virginia, USA

About once a month someone sends me a link to a video of a deaf person being activated with a cochlear implant and hearing for the first time. There is that moment after the implant is activated and everyone is crying tears of joy. It is assumed the cochlear implant is like a "magic wand" that restores perfect hearing instantly. For some that activation experience can happen, depending on the type of hearing loss they have.

I thought this would be my experience as well on my activation day. I waited with such excited anticipation with all kinds of happy scenes dancing in my head. Like Dorothy in the Wizard of Oz stepping out of the black & white and walking into a world of beautiful color. Like the "water scene" in The Miracle Worker, when Helen had an epiphany that everything had a name. But it was no happy scene for me. When that switch turned on, I was shocked. It's a noisy world!

People don't understand that it's lot of work to learn to hear with a bionic device. Suppose that you were blind all of your life and suddenly you could see. Do you think your brain would instantly make sense the world around you? It's the same with hearing. Returning to work post activation was not easy. In the break room conversation competed with noises of the microwave humming, refrigerator buzzing, water facet running, coke machine clanging, coffee machine percolating and the droning heat system. Voices sounded like cartoon characters.

It was frightening as a musician because music sounded like a tangled mess of disembodied pitches in a fevered dream. I play for hospital patients and at nursing homes. One day a woman shouted at me "You can't play and you can't sing!" I was stunned because I thought, "maybe she is right?"

Some weeks after my activation, I began working with Alia Juvonen, a music teacher and doing some ear training exercises. We worked with tuning forks to aid me in feeling the vibrations of the pitches & frequencies of notes. In one exercise she quizzed me on interval recognition. (An interval is a combination of two notes, or the distance between their pitches.) She would play two notes in succession and I would listen to see if I could discern what interval it was. There are song charts that can be found online one can use as an aid with interval recognition. Some examples are: first measure of "Twinkle, Twinkle Little Star" has a perfect fifth, the intro to "When the Saints Go Marching In" is a major third, "Somewhere Over the Rainbow" begins with an octave, and so on. The reason this is a significant exercise is because intervals are what make up a melody. The idea being that if you are able to distinguish pitches by isolating them as we did in the above exercise that can improve your ability to discern notes in a melody.

Other things we did were from a book called, "Sight Singing: Pitch, Interval, Rhythm" by Samuel Adler. In these exercises, we worked with the piano and guitar, sounding the notes of the intervals and then singing them a cappella. The goal of these exercises was the pretty much the same as above, to be able to discern intervals and to also produce them by singing. In more advanced drills, we would start by singing a series of notes in a melody out loud and then read the notes in our head silently and at the last measure of the line, sing the notes out loud again and then check with the piano to see if we stayed on pitch. It was all a lot of fun and also very challenging. I believe that doing these exercises really helped me regain my musical perception. My music teacher said that even most musicians don't do these sorts of exercises, but because many people who play an instrument hear melodies without a problem, they don't feel the need to. I get emails from CI users all over the country asking how it is I am able to hear a melody. I hope what I described above will be helpful to others.

Six months after my activation in February 2009, I got a new digital hearing aid (Phonak Naida) for my right ear. It was then I really experienced a miracle for I could then hear every note on my guitar. Before my CI and HA I could hear up to the 7th fret but now I could hear every note, all the way to the 19th fret. However, I disliked the sound quality of the hearing aid. Everything sounded kind of metallic and unnatural. Today, I no longer use my hearing aid and rely solely on my Nucleus 6 cochlear implant.

Two years post activation, I was able to leave my job as an administrative assistant and pursue my lifelong dream to become a professional musician. I am employed at the University of Virginia Hospital as a Certified Music Practitioner where I play therapeutic music at the bedside. In addition, I work for Very Special Arts (VSA) in Charlottesville, which is an international organization dedicated to promote experiences in the arts for individuals with disabilities. I have one CD recording to my credit, "Choose the Sky" that was completed in 2011. As the recording took 5 years to complete (having to take a break during my CI rehab), it was part hard work, part inspiring achievement, and part miracle. I also play for weddings and conferences and all kinds of special events. I love to meet new people, so feel free to get in touch! Website: http://blueoconnell.com/

Janice Rosen

Janice Rosen—Piano, clarinet and voice student
Washington, DC, USA

I was born with normal hearing, but have malformed middle ear bones that did not grow properly and I started losing my hearing slowly as a toddler. By age 6 even though my hearing loss was mild, it was severe enough that I needed to wear hearing aids to function normally.

I began learning to sing at age 3 or earlier from my Dad, who was not a professional musician, but just someone who loved music and had a good voice. I have also loved listening to the Metropolitan Opera radio broadcasts ever since I was an infant and when I would hear the bel canto sopranos, I would try to sing along.

I sang in my synagogue youth choir and had a very supportive choir director / music teacher who would train all of us children how to sing properly, with breathing exercises and scales. My hearing aids helped me hear but my problem was in knowing how loud I would be in comparison with the others in the choir. I had to listen carefully to everyone else and watch the choir director. It helped that she would sing along mouthing the words and I would lip-read in order to make sure I was keeping proper time and keeping up with everyone. I sang alto and most of the time the altos would sing very softly, too softly. I could hear the sopranos better---maybe because they were louder.

Piano was frustrating when I was younger not because of hearing but because of my bimanual synkinesis (congenital mirror movement syndrome), involuntary mirroring of the opposite hand muscles. This makes learning to play the piano difficult but not impossible. I did not take formal piano lessons when I was a child even though I wanted to very much. I did enjoy playing around on my family's organ and inventing melodies with one hand.

When my family would visit friends who had a piano, the piano was where I would head to first and start playing my one-handed inventions for everyone.

I found it easier to learn to play the clarinet and recorder, as it was not necessary to have good hand coordination (at least not as much so as on a piano). I played clarinet in my high school band and also some clarinet and recorder solos in programs at my synagogue when I was a teenager.

In high school I took the Seashore Test of Musical Ability and did very well but both my high school band teacher and my guidance counselor were very negative. They did not want me playing in the high school marching band and said that I should not think about a career in music due to my hearing loss.

In 2001, the Association of Adult Musicians with Hearing Loss (AAMHL) was founded and that opened up a whole new world for me as an amateur musician and music lover.

One of the things I learned about through AAMHL is the Note Frequency Conversion Chart on the AAMHL website which indicates what frequency each note on a piano keyboard is. It was what I needed in assisting me in choosing my first digital hearing aids in 2002. I showed the chart to my hearing aid dealer / audiologist and shared with him that I wanted to be able to hear all the frequencies on a piano as well as the full range of the human singing voice – assuming that I have the auditory nerves to allow me to do this. There are no musical instruments or music testing equipment in the hearing aid dealer's office so he tested my hearing, programmed the hearing aids based on my audiogram and the Note Frequency Conversion Chart.

As I live only a short distance away from his office, I went home and tried listening to the notes on my piano and CD's of singers I enjoy (especially Joan Sutherland) in order determining if the sound is in fact "just right." I also tested the hearing aids by listening to my favorite opera singers at the Washington National Opera. This was an especially useful environmental test with the bel canto and the flourishing coloratura singers that I know so well. However, this is not a very scientific test and I know that even with the best hearing aids I am not hearing music the same way someone with normal hearing is.

My current hearing aids are Widex Super 440 with the receiver in the ear molds very close to the eardrums. Because of the way the sound is transmitted to my eardrums, middle ears, and inner ear nerves (mostly via bone conduction), my singing ability has improved, as well as my piano and clarinet playing. I also have good teachers who are able to meet my voice, hearing, and physical challenges where they are and to help me learn how to use what I have and to do what I need to do to make good sound, whether I am singing, playing the piano or the clarinet.

Thanks to AAMHL and the many fine people and resources I have come in contact with, I have been able to revitalize my love and pursuit of music as an avocation. My greatest musical passion is the art of classical singing and I hope some day to do some work in the area of teaching or research on singing for people who have a hearing loss.

Stephen Shey

Stephen Shey—Violinist, violin and piano teacher
Boston, Massachusetts, USA

I began my journey with music at the age of 3 on a makeshift Cracker Jack box violin. I started my violin training with the Suzuki method, an approach to learning music that is heavily based on listening to recordings. I remember listening nonstop to the repertoire I was learning at the time. Every time I was in the car I was listening to my cassette player with headphones.

It was not until I was 5 years old that my family and I learned that I was hard of hearing through a hearing test done at school. From that moment on, my life changed drastically. So many questions were finally answered! Up until that point my family thought I was just absent-minded or just not focused, because I kept saying, "what?" or not responding and giving them a blank stare. I was taken out of my class and placed into a special education class. I was instantly hooked up to a FM receiver, and naturally the dynamics at school changed.

That same year, my family relocated from the Washington DC area to the suburbs of Boston and then we learned that I have bilateral hearing loss, with my left ear having more hearing loss than my right ear. Not too long after moving to the Boston area, hearing aids and FM receivers became a regular routine of school and daily life. Hearing aids back then were not as discreet nor were they as technologically advanced as they are now, so when it came to practicing violin or performances, I took out my hearing aids. I took them out because the analog hearing aid would emit a static-like sound because it could not process the higher frequencies or it amplified the violin sound even more and became too loud.

By the time I was 9 years old, my parents had enrolled me at the New England Conservatory (NEC) preparatory school. Even at this age, I dreamed of becoming a concert violinist. As my desire to becoming a professional violinist grew, the amount of time I was spending with my violin increased day after day.

I was very self-conscious about wearing hearing aids, whether at school or outside of school. I felt that there was a magnifying glass on me when I wore hearing aids. Through elementary school, hearing aids and FM receivers were only used for academic/school purposes. The moment I got home I took out my hearing aids and left them out, regardless of whether I was practicing or not. Oddly enough around this time, I discovered that I had developed perfect pitch. I believe that I was able to develop this partly through the Suzuki approach of listening to repertoire constantly and associating pitch to kinesthetic movement, and also by being hyper-aware of how my hands/fingers moved to create certain notes.

My insecurity and self-consciousness with having to wear hearing aids overrode the understanding and realization of the benefits of wearing them. Because of this my academics began declining, as did my overall growth with the violin. In the classroom, despite sitting in the front row, I would not be able to catch everything the teacher said. This was especially noticeable if the teacher turned their back to me to write something on the chalkboard. Although I had access to an FM system in the regular public school classroom, many times my teachers were not used to using the FM transmitter. They would forget to turn the transmitter on, or not secure the lapel mic properly to their clothing. As a result, I often missed bits and parts of explanations and this left holes in my learning and understanding. I was too shy, insecure, and embarrassed to ask my teachers to repeat what they had just said.

On Saturdays at NEC Preparatory, I began to slack off in auditions to assure that I would not be concertmaster or as the principal in the second violin section, knowing that I would not be able to hear the conductor and make adjustments on the fly despite being seated only 3 feet away.

I began to skip music theory classes because it was another classroom setting where I could not hear too well because more often than not, the teachers' back was turned to me as they were constantly writing things down on the chalkboard and I had no idea how to decipher what they were writing.

My parents finally enrolled me in a small private school when I started sixth grade, and I finally ditched my hearing aids completely. I was trying as hard as possible to look "normal", and it felt so good to be respected for what I could do on the soccer field and in the school orchestra, instead of being seen as the hearing-impaired boy who did not hear well in a large public school and needed to use hearing aids. For the next 12 years I went without wearing hearing aids, and learned to read lips enough to fill gaps. I relied on my eyes to try and make up for what I was not hearing, and I became very observant of body language in conversations. In music ensemble situations, I would memorize my part as much as I could so my eyes could keenly watch the pianists' fingers as they pressed the keys, or the cellists' bows when they made contact with the strings during a musical piece we were working on.

Through the love, support, and encouragement from my family and friends, I finally sought out my current hearing aid, the Oticon Agil Pro. For the last 5 years I have been wearing my left hearing aid every day, and it has wondrously changed my interactions and communication with others.

It has made me more confident about participating in conversations fully and not only rely on reading lips and body language to gauge the tone and temperament of the conversation. I look forward to experiencing the continued advancements in hearing aid technology. I am excited and hopeful that hearing aids will evolve to the point where they will be like glasses and I will one day have 20/20 hearing.

Esther Sokol

Making Music with a Hearing Loss: Strategies and Stories

Esther Sokol—Pianist
Alpharetta, Georgia, USA

I had inherited, along with my two older brothers, the family hearing loss gene from my mother's side. I attribute its physical onset to psychological trauma: my husband died unexpectedly at age 37, leaving me with three young children ages 5, 7 and 9. I was 35 years old at that time. A couple of years later, my supervisor at work took me aside and suggested I get my hearing checked. A stapedectomy was unsuccessful, as well as a revision surgery. Then followed the physical trauma of having my ear being fitted with a foreign ear mold and first hearing aid in the right ear, and then a second hearing aid the left ear.

My mother's wedding gift, an Ivers & Pond upright piano from Boston, stood next to my father's favorite chair in our small parlor. After a day's hard work, he would sink into his chair and listen the familiar Hebrew songs he loved. I started picking out the musical notes from the songs at around age 5; my piano lessons started at age 7. I studied applied music/piano performance at the New England Conservatory at 14, graduated from Boston University College of Music, earned the Master of Arts in Teaching at Harvard, then was awarded a Wooley Scholarship in France (Paris Conservatory). After graduation, I studied with Arthur Loesser at the Cleveland Institute of Music; I currently attend university music classes in Atlanta, Georgia. During my 20+ years working in New York City, my piano was in storage; upon retirement, I returned to the piano and discovered chamber music. Resettled in Atlanta, I continue to study privately and also teach in my private studio. A master technician tunes my Yamaha grand piano; he is my "ears."

Chamber music is my passion! Since 2008, I have performed at annual chamber music workshops for advanced musicians. The auditory challenge, especially for a hard of hearing pianist, is to balance with the other parts--in duos, trios, quartets, quintets. The hearing aid challenge is to make/hear acoustic music with less-than–perfect digital hearing aids. The classical masterpieces deserve no less than lifelong study.

A hard of hearing pianist--even this "experienced listener"--faces many different challenges. First, our instruments (and voices) are affected by temperature and humidity. I don't carry mine around! So every piano I play sounds and feels different in its place. The lid may be lowered, raised--or even closed, accordingly. My aided-ears, my arms may hear and feel forte but in actuality blends in with the other players' mezzo forte. Conversely, my piano may not come through in a dolce or accompaniment passage. All the while I am reading thousands of notes, using 10 fingers and most all my senses, from head to toe! It is definitely a lot of work.

Communicating with normal-hearing musicians in chamber music situations can be a problem. Whether in small or large ensembles, we communicate vocally during rehearsals and with visual cues during performance. We are continually listening to each other's sounds. Seating arrangement is important. The only one I may be facing across the piano may be a clarinetist or violist. The cellist sits at an angle facing the audience near the curve of the piano; I watch for the down bow. I prefer the violinist to be seated on a line with the piano bench, in my peripheral vision where I can watch for a down bow. A true ensemble "feel" is when I can turn toward the soloist in the next passage, and smile that we are holding the group together. We are projecting beautiful music to an appreciative audience—all of us listening (to Beethoven) together!

Venue acoustics also pose another problem. Different performance venues present different hearing environments, sometimes presenting rude surprises. "Dead" practice rooms. Carpeted living rooms. Full (hopefully) concert halls. Large performance spaces. What's a hard of hearing musician to do during rehearsals when the coach is saying something to us from the first row in the audience and I strain to hear from the empty stage?

The limits of today's hearing technology pose another challenge. My current hearing aids must be as good as possible for making and listening to acoustic music---that is, my basic speech program. "Music programs" in hearing aids are designed for listening to music recordings, not for hearing or performing live, acoustic music. Most audiologists don't realize that. My 40+ years of hearing loss is now almost off the charts, and still I suffer the anxiety of having to replace my best-ever Oticon Atlas baseline-digital aids (which are no longer being made). Truth be told, they are not at the back of the drawer but still serve as my backup aids. As I understand it, manufacturers have not spent on research in the past five-plus years to make improvements in hearing aids for musicians, a small population to them. Musicians with hearing loss should be sure to seek out an experienced audiologist who has musician clients!

Assistive listening devices also pose some challenges. I struggle to explain to my piano coach that I hear my music on his 7-foot concert grand yet strain to catch his words, sitting just a few feet away. Clicking back and forth using assistive listening devices (transmitters/receivers) just can't keep up with our quick exchanges in chamber groups; it interrupts the flow of the music. The extra seconds of waiting is tiring and trying, and makes us all not as patient and accommodating, as we would like to be. I consider my eyeglasses to be an assistive listening device! Lighting is important. Videotaped playbacks can be helpful, even surprising.

For me, the Association of Adult Musicians with Hearing Loss was a welcome discovery and resource---everyone who contributes to this resource benefits. I realized how fortunate I am to have had normal hearing until age 37 and to have accomplished much in my second career as a "returning pianist."

Angelika Wild

(photo by J. Burger)

Angelika Wild—Cellist
Hinterbrühl, Austria

In the summer of 2013, a sudden loss of hearing led to major upheavals in my life as a professional musician. Per my doctor's orders, I stopped playing cello---I have been playing cello since I was five years old--- and underwent drug therapy to stop the hearing loss. After a few days, the left ear recovered completely, but the right ear was permanently damaged. I also experienced tinnitus in the right ear and became extremely sensitive to noise.

In addition, my hearing loss now posed significant challenges in ensemble situations. Sitting in the cello section during orchestra rehearsals, my impaired right ear could no longer hear the violas to confirm rhythm of the music we played while the left ear (which was closer to the audience) provided no auditory assistance or cues. I started paying more attention to the body language of the musicians around me as a way to compensate for the auditory deficit in the right ear. A second, more serious problem appeared when I discovered I was having great difficulties hearing the conductor's instructions or comments by my fellow members in the ensemble during rehearsals.

Early in 2015, I made the decision to look for ways to improve my hearing situation. Since my hearing loss is mostly in the higher frequencies, I researched the internet for an audiologist who specializes in working with musicians. I was able to locate an audiologist who had studied sound engineering at the University of Music and Performing Arts in Vienna. It is comforting to be able to describe musical timbre and acoustic perceptions to someone who can understand the technical jargon we musicians use.

At my second visit with my audiologist where I got to try my first hearing aid, I was overwhelmed with emotion . . . it felt so good to be able to hear again with two ears. After a total of 10 sessions over four months experimenting with different settings and changes to the hearing aid, I was satisfied and really happy to have found a technical solution to my problem. I am now able to differentiate between speech input and music input. I can now understand the conductor again. I have regained the quality of life I had before my sudden hearing loss and my feelings of depression have eased.

Overall, I am happy with my experience of obtaining a hearing aid. I am of the opinion though, that while having the expertise of a skilled audiologist is essential, it is also necessary that new hearing aid users be patient and be prepare to work closely with the audiologist over a period of time to get the hearing aid settings to be the way you want. Each person's hearing loss is complex and unique.

"I'm not a deaf musician. I am a musician who happens to be deaf."

Evelyn Glennie, Scottish percussionist

Nancy M. Williams

Nancy M. Williams—Pianist, Speaker, Hearing Loss Advocate
Fairfield, Connecticut, USA

For years, my love of the piano and fear of my hearing loss were intimately intertwined. Although I was diagnosed with a genetic hearing loss at age six, I did not receive my first hearing aid until I was in seventh grade, several years after I began studying the piano. I couldn't get enough time on the piano; when I wasn't practicing, I craved the dulcet sound of the keys. At age 15, I performed a Rachmaninoff Prelude in recital. Then family and financial pressures forced me to quit not long afterwards. I was told that with a hearing loss, I would never be a concert pianist. From that point forward, I tried to hide my loss, wearing my hair long to cover my hearing aids. The profile of my slowly worsened over the years, inching down the audiogram, so that by the time I turned 40, I had a moderate loss, sloping to severe in the high frequencies. Yet that year, I found my way back to the piano, enrolling in adult piano lessons. A decade later, I have become a performing amateur pianist, speaker, hearing health advocate, and founding editor of the website Grand Piano Passion™. During this decade of transformation, one experience at a packed piano recital was crucial in my development.

When I went back to the piano in my early forties, I decided not to mention my genetic hearing loss to my teacher, Stephen. He might conclude that I was slow, out of touch, even thickheaded, certainly unlikely to realize my goal of reclaiming the piano. I couldn't know that eventually my denial of my hearing loss would catch up with me in a public domain, a piano recital.

My hearing aids were the kind that audiologists refer to as half shells, the shape of two tiny apples protruding from my ears. I hoped Stephen wouldn't notice my aids—after all, they were flesh-colored—even on days when I wore my long hair pulled back. One time during my lesson, after I struck some booming, forte chords, my aids whistled in the soundproofed practice room. I cringed. What kind of serious piano student would have to contend with colicky hearing aids? Stephen, who had acute hearing, no doubt detected the squeaking.

One day at my lesson, I took a deep breath. "I should tell you I wear hearing aids."

"I noticed," Stephen said. "Can you hear all the notes on the piano?"

"With my hearing aids on, yes. Except these high notes…" I ran my fingers down the top octave.

Stephen nodded with a thoughtful encouragement. "It doesn't seem to affect your playing. You're very musical."

His response felt like a blessing.

After a blissful four years of piano lessons with Stephen, studying composers like Chopin, Debussy, and Schumann,, I invested in a new pair of hearing aids—miniature pears, delicate, and so petite that only their flat bottoms could be glimpsed in my outer ear canals. On the shell's exteriors were tiny buttons, which I pressed to access different settings, one beep inside my ear for everyday conversation, two for talking on the phone, and most miraculously, three beeps for playing the piano.

Yet at my weekly piano lesson, I usually forgot to switch to the music setting. Several bars into my piece, the aids' tiny microchips, still programmed to the main setting and therefore fixated on amplifying conversation, would decide that the piano sounds ought to remain in the background. Inside my ears, the music would assume a flat, muffled character.

Yet I had years of experience wearing hearing aids—I had received my first hearing aid in seventh grade, a banana-shaped, behind-the-ear model, connected to an ear mold with clear plastic tubing, which I often pressed down, hoping to make less obtrusive. My forgetfulness about the music setting seemed odd, even flighty.

In the spring, Stephen held a recital for his students at Crane's Mill Retirement Community. My turn to perform came at the end of the program. A hundred people—family, including my husband and two children, along with residents of the retirement community—sat in rows of folding chairs that stretched to the hall's rear doors.

I launched into Chopin's "Raindrop Prelude." The opening melody was ruminative, almost rapt. A few measures in, the music

Making Music with a Hearing Loss: Strategies and Stories

lost its shimmering quality, the tones becoming dull and smothered.

Perhaps the harsh, dry winter had done in the piano. Or could it be that during the last couple of days my hearing had worsened? After my pinky reached for a low A-flat in the bass, I realized with a sickening clarity that I had forgotten to toggle my aids to the music setting.

I could not fake my way through five minutes of the Prelude without hearing the piano's full richness of sound. Yet if I were to stop, tap my aids' buttons, and begin the music anew, people in the audience would know that I wore hearing aids. A panicky adrenaline buzzed within me; I felt at a loss on how to fix my situation.

I plowed through the next measure, where the Prelude's opening melody assumed a tender variation. People in the audience would know that I wore hearing aids. Despite that so many people were watching me, I could admit to myself that I continually forgot to switch to the music setting because I wanted to pretend that my aids did not exist and that my hearing was normal. I had allowed stereotypes of people with hearing loss—slow, out of touch, thickheaded—and the stigma against hearing aids to mildew within. I was ashamed of my loss.

I stopped playing. I pressed the buttons on my hearing aids, heard the three perky tones signifying the music setting, and sighed with relief. I stood up from the bench. I strode towards the microphone, self-conscious and brazen at the same time. Several people in the audience looked stricken, as though mortified on my behalf. Yet for me the humiliation already had happened, during all of the years I tried to hide an undeniable part of myself.

"I wear hearing aids," I said into the microphone. "And I forgot to turn on the music setting. I'm going to try again."

The audience clapped, a few people stomping their feet, in encouragement. I sat down at the piano, inhaled a slow, deep breath, and sang the first bar in my mind, as though I were beginning the "Raindrop Prelude" for the first time. When I touched my fingers to the keys, sound floated around me, resonant, textured, and fully heard.

Nobuyuki Yoshimoto

Nobuyuki Yoshimoto—String bassist and guitarist
Shimonoseki, Japan

I was born in Fukuoka, Japan in 1957. While in studying in college, I developed an interest in jazz music. I picked up the string bass and guitar and have been playing as a semi-professional musician since then. Around 1990, I started experiencing hearing loss in my right ear and eventually lost all my hearing in that ear. As for my left ear, I was having a hard time hearing high-pitched sounds and was experiencing constant dizziness. Playing music under these conditions was extremely difficult; however, I was determined to keep playing music. I have recorded 4 CDs under the name "Dizzy Yoshimoto" which is available in Japan. My third CD, titled "HAPPINESS" became very popular and was the best-selling album for two weeks on "kakaku.com", which is an online shopping website in Japan.

In 2012, I lost the remaining hearing in my left ear and became completely deaf. I was forced to stop playing music at this point. In 2014, I underwent cochlear implant surgery in my left ear. After some rehabilitation, I was able to hear metallic sounds and some high-pitched sounds. I was also able to understand some face-to-face conversation, supplemented by lip reading. As far as playing music goes, I am still unable to recognize notes, melody, harmony and intervals. Currently I am performing in various musical events and clubs as a "jazz bassist and guitarist with a cochlear implant".

How can I play jazz when I cannot hear music? Especially when improvisation is the most important part of jazz music? For other genres of music, if you play as it is written on a musical score, music is created. However, in jazz music, you only have the chords and melody of the theme written in the chart. The rest is improvised by the instrumentalist(s) and that makes up the tune. In improvisation, you are expected to play a solo according to the song's chord progression in a certain style of jazz phrasing, such as bebop. In order to achieve this, you have to listen and memorize the phrasing of many great players, such as Charlie Parker, Miles Davis, and John Coltrane, who we call "Giants of Jazz".

Then, you have to come up with your own phrasing. If you cannot hear music, you cannot learn from these great players. As I cannot recognize notes, melody, harmony and intervals, it is extremely difficult to play the exact phrase that I came up in my head on my instrument without writing on the chart. However I overcame this difficulty by relying on my past experiences as a jazz musician. I know so many tunes and have memorized many, many songs, so I am able to come up with my own phrasing and can sing it. I can play most of jazz standards now because of my continuous efforts of practicing with metronome and my past experience of playing instruments. As for the improvisation, I am able to play solo with "jazz phrasing", even though it may not be perfect. Even though I am not able to hear music, having a cochlear implant has made it possible to hear metallic and environmental sounds. As a result, I am able to practice with a metronome. I have been training myself everyday by playing a tune that I know well in various tempos and rhythmic patterns with a metronome. Now I'm able to play music with others while keeping a steady rhythm.

There are a few different methods for practicing with a metronome. For example, if the time signature of the tune is in 4/4 time, I will set the metronome to click on the 2 and 4 beat. If the tune is in ¾ time, I set it to click on beat 3 only. There are other ways to set metronome to click in different places. Continuous practicing is extremely important so you are able play in an exact tempo with various rhythmic patterns. Another very important thing is to memorize the tune so you can play without reading the chart. Except when I'm practicing, I cannot look at the chart, because I need to see what other musicians are doing. Playing in an ensemble requires your attention for what other instrumentalists are doing; otherwise you cannot play "in sync" with them, since I cannot hear well what other musicians are playing. In order to achieve my goal, my daily training includes (1) practicing with metronome (2) memorize jazz tunes (3) play improvised phrases on my instruments (upright bass, guitar and piano).

It is extremely difficult to play jazz music when I am unable to hear or recognize and melodies, or hear the sound of the instrument I'm playing on. However, it is possible to "feel" the music by imagining the sound in my head. Daily training is a must to achieve this, but it is rewarding when I feel like "I'm playing together" with other musicians.

This feeling of being in sync with other musicians is awesome and I am so glad that I did not stop playing jazz music. The cochlear implant made it possible to hear certain sounds; I am so thankful for being able to hear that much and deeply appreciate the support from I receive from my friends and patrons of my jazz bar. I am determined to keep practicing in order to play jazz music.

Jay Alan Zimmerman

(photo by B. Norman)

Jay Alan Zimmerman—Composer, pianist, and visual music artist

New York, New York, USA

In my family, making music was the main entertainment and our favorite way to have fun together. Mom taught piano and music theory at our local college in Iowa, Dad sang tenor in the church choir and local musicals, and my two siblings played instruments in band as well as sang. We'd have whistling competitions, sing rounds on car trips, and even perform together as family singers... sort of like the Von Trapp family from the "Sound of Music" but probably not as good. So with my childhood bed upstairs directly over Mom's grand piano, music being family playtime, and my hearing considered "normal" into my late 20s -- I simply cannot recall a single day without making music, even with profound deafness. I started regular piano lessons at age 5; saxophone at 8; and jazz piano in junior high school. I played oboe in high school band and rang handbells at church. I played with big bands, jazz bands, marching bands and orchestras. I sang as a boy soprano in musicals, church choirs and school choruses. Later, I sang tenor in "swing choir", musicals, and served as soloist for the Messiah during holiday performances.

After moving to New York City, I was able to publish my first children's songbook and scored a London production before finishing up college at New York University. How and why I started losing my hearing may always remain a mystery, but the last straw was my proximity and exposure to the tragedy of September 11th, 2001 in New York City. The dust exposure caused numerous sinus issues, which have been linked to hearing loss, and both the noise exposure, and the ototoxicity of components in the dust has finally been documented. But clearly something made me susceptible to it, causing the initial high frequency loss that made my manager send me to a doctor, as well as allowing the 9/11 exposures to push me over the edge into profound deafness.

Currently, audiology tests say I have virtually no hearing above 250hz (middle C) but I feel I am sensing something of those higher frequencies at times, perhaps through bone vibration.

Below 250hz--which is not usually measured by audiologists--the last test said I was at 60db. It's this tiny little corner of sound that I use to create music, employing amplification apps to boost the frequencies I can still perceive. But amplification loses its benefits after a few hours due to pain and exhaustion so I try to use all my other senses more fully--ears, eyes, body, and mind.

The mind is the most powerful tool because we hear with our brains and can build up a vast sound memory just like some people have photographic memories. I feel very fortunate that my musical background allowed me to build up a large mental library of sound. The eyes are also great for visual representations of music like music scores, music visualizers, frequency analysis, and even lipreading and sign language. But it's very difficult to represent the nuance, complexity, and specificity of music with today's visual aids. The body too is a great tool as a receiver of vibrations and I've just begun to explore this avenue. It's the combination of all these tools together that allows me to keep creating music.

Because I'm a musician first and a social person second, my choices for dealing with hearing loss have been unique and not always respected by the medical community. Their emphasis is on speech comprehension because obviously that's what most people need and want. My emphasis is on music elements: pitch accuracy, stereo perception, harmony and timbre discrimination. Hearing aids were not successful for me even with mild/moderate loss, but I used amplification daily via headphones and equalizers. I've often considered cochlear implants, but rejected them because of their current lack of pitch/timbre discrimination.

This makes me quite an outlier. But I've found embracing my "deaf" side to be freeing. Music will always be with me no matter what my ears can discern. My hope is to use my life experience and this odd journey through assistive technology to better understand others, and myself and to transform this understanding into meaningful art.

And, oh yeah, I want to create at least one musical that makes it to Broadway!

Appendices

APPENDIX I

Frequency to Musical Note Converter

Frequency (sharp/flat)	Frequency (natural)	Note name
	4186.0	C8
	3951.1	B7
3729.3	3520.0	A7
3322.4	3136.0	A7
2960.0	2793.8	G7
	2637.0	F7
2489.0	2349.3	E7
2217.5	2093.0	D7
	1975.5	C7
1864.7	1760.0	B6
1661.2	1568.0	A6
1480.0	1396.9	G6
	1318.5	F6
1244.5	1174.7	E6
1108.7	1046.5	D6
	987.77	C6
932.33	880.00	B5
830.61	783.99	A5
739.99	698.46	G5
	659.26	F5
622.25	587.33	E5
554.37	523.25	D5
	493.88	C5
466.16	**440.0**	B4
415.30	392.00	**A4**
369.99	349.23	G4
	329.63	F4
311.13	293.67	E4
277.18	**261.6**	D4
	246.94	**C4**
233.08	220.00	B3
207.65	196.00	A3
185.00	174.61	G3
	164.81	F3
155.56	146.83	E3
138.59	130.81	D3
	123.47	C3
116.54	110.00	B2
103.83	97.999	A2
92.499	87.307	G2
	82.407	F2
77.782	73.416	E2
69.296	65.406	D2
	61.735	C2
58.270	55.000	B1
51.913	48.999	A1
46.249	43.654	G1
	41.203	F1
38.891	36.708	E1
34.648	32.703	D1
	30.868	C1
29.135	27.500	B0
		A0

J. Wolfe, UNSW

Diagram courtesy of the Music Acoustics Dept, School of Physics, University of New South Wales, Sydney, Australia. (www.phys.unsw.edu.au/jw/notes.html). Used with permission.

Print Resources

Behar, A., Chasin, M., and Cheesman, M., *Noise Control: A Primer.* Singular Publishing Group: San Diego, California (September 1999). ISBN# 1565939921.

Chasin, Marshall, (Editor). *CIC Handbook*, Singular Publishing Group: San Diego, California (Sept. 1997). ISBN# 1565938291.

_____, *Hear the Music: Hearing Loss Prevention for Musicians.* Self published: Toronto, Canada (2001). Currently 4th edition. ISBN# 0920445748.

_____, (Editor), *Hearing Loss in Musicians: Prevention and Management.* Plural Publishing Inc., (2009). ISBN# 9781597561815.

_____, *Musicians and the Prevention of Hearing Loss.* Singular Publishing Group: San Diego, California, (April 1996). ISBN#156593624.

_____, (Editor), *Consumer Handbook on Hearing Loss in Noise.* Auricle Ink Publishing: Sedona, Arizona (March 2010). ISBN# 978-09825785-06.

Levitin, Daniel J, *This is Your Brain On Music: The Science of a Human Obsession.* Penguin Group Publishers: NY, NY (2007). ISBN# 978-0452288522.

Internet Sources

American Academy of Audiology (AAA).
http://www.asha.org/
Professional organization for audiologists. Contains information for consumers on hearing loss.

Association for Adult Musicians with Hearing Loss (AAMHL).
http://musicianswithhearingloss.org
Network of amateur and professional musicians, audiologists, and music educators with significant hearing loss. Online listserv forum and Facebook group for discussions regarding how music is perceived and performed with current hearing aid and cochlear implant technology.

Better Hearing Institute
http://www.betterhearing.org/
Comprehensive information on hearing loss, tinnitus, and hearing aids.

Grand Piano Passion
http://www.grandpianopassion.com/category/hearing-music/
musicians-with-hearing-loss/
Grand Piano Passion is a blog founded by pianist Nancy M. Williams. There are many articles that discusses making music with a hearing loss.

Hear the Music
http://hearinghealthmatters.org/hearthemusic
Dr. Marshall Chasin maintains a blog about music and hearing perception. Many blog entries are of interest to musicians with hearing loss.

Hearing Loss Association of America (HLAA).
http://www.hearingloss.org/
The leading organization representing consumers with hearing loss in the United States.

Journey into the World of Hearing
http://www.cochlea.org/en/hear/music-perception
Informative tutorial about the inner ear from the laboratory of
Rémy Pujol in Montpellier. France. This site replaced the old
"Promenade Around the Cochlea" tutorial.

Musicians Clinics of Canada (MCC)
http://www.musiciansclinics.com/
This is Dr. Marshall Chasin's clinic website.

Say What Club
http:www.saywhatclub.com/
Worldwide forum for individuals with hearing loss

NOTES

33648142R00077

Made in the USA
Middletown, DE
21 July 2016